# Wheels of Witchcraft

# WHEELS OF WITCHCRAFT
A Biker Witch's Guide to Riding the Mystical Path

*Author*
**Rhiannon Redpath**

*Editor*
**Serena Doyle**

*Illustrator*
**Chloe Owen**

*Foreword by*
**Pixie Lighthorse**

Concluded in the year 2025.
Written upon Bulbancha, the place of many tongues.
Where the spirit of this book rises in reclamation,
its many voices weaving a living melody of ancient magic.

Written and published by Rhiannon Redpath

Motherline Magic LLC

New Orleans, Louisiana

www.motherlinemagic.com

ISBN: 979-8-218-77279-6

In keeping with the Motherline Magic Moto Coven's ethos of reciprocity, a portion of the profits from *Wheels of Witchcraft* is contributed to the New Orleans–based organization, Common Ground Relief. Through this offering, we support their work in restoring the wetlands and strengthening the New Orleans community that we are privileged to be part of. Our presence in these lands carries a responsibility, and this is one way we honor that sacred connection.

*For you, Mom, because you deserved better.*

*Keep the fire hot and the beer cold.*

*I'll see you on the other side.*

*I love you.*

# THE ROAD AHEAD

# Foreword

Rhiannon and I met in New Orleans to walk and talk, to wade quickly into the deep end of all swampy matters before we'd gotten half way through the Quarter. I was immediately struck by her tenderness and connectedness—how she smiled admiringly toward my fifteen year old daughter as we wove our way down the bustling sidewalks.

My daughter strode out ahead of us, shoulders squared, chin high, leading the way forward in her signature shredded safety-pinned jeans, Cramps tee shirt, and Sharpie tattoos on her hands. She was riding high on her first trip to our beautiful, ancestral homelands along Atchafalaya at Christmastime.

We watched her and listened to her that afternoon, multitasking as we do, turning over the logs of our own childhoods under moss-dripping oaks and flocks of intriguing birds.

Who Rhiannon saw that day was the walking example of what happens when a daughter has an emotionally resourced mother who is able to support her development and nurture her confidence. Unlike Rhiannon and I, my daughter has a mother we do not have.

Women carry our mothers' heartbreaks and limited capacities. We cling to their bedtime songs, their loving gestures, their scents. It is hard to have never had these acts of care, and also hard to have had them for a too-short time. It is a longing that will never leave me.

Mothering a daughter has been a bittersweet tour along snaking roadways through steep canyons, my own mother's faults and failures stalking me around every curve. Some of our mothers are not able to be in this world anymore. Some are, and can't offer us healing they haven't been able to come to.

The wounds of motherness shape us all. There is pressure from all sides of society for women to do this particular job correctly from beginning to end, with little room for mistakes and our own pressing issues to tend.

Between the demands of purity culture that favors modesty in women and distorted feminism—the kind that deceives women into believing that standing up to patriarchy means participating on its terms to ensure a secure place in the culture—we are not yet able to experience the liberation our foremothers fought for.

We who came through matrilineal tribes are among the few. For most, it has been many, many generations since women in your lineage held real power. This can mean the legacy burdens you're carrying are too bulky to strap to a sissy bar and lug across the lands.

Nothing inspires courage, healing, liberation, and freedom more than lightening our loads. There are many hours for asking the ride to release us, allow our mother's songs to come up through us, to hum them like cherished secrets inside our helmets, soothing in the ways she would have liked to, but perhaps couldn't.

For many women and femmes, riding motorcycles occupies yet another space reserved for and dominated by cis-hetereo men. Today's rider is invited to challenge narratives of patriarchal power hoarding used to subordinate other groups with less agency. We can always leverage privilege to uplift others, and this work is a clear invitation to examine who we are as women on the map in this space and time.

Motorcycle riding is a metaphor for how we go along on the path of life, it's how we *get ourselves there*. The road is earth, our shared Mother, who is always revealing her medicines to heal the lineages, to bring home after the journey to share with the people. To do this creates paths for others coming up behind you. The highway, trial, and trail are opportunities to create corrective experiences and learn to more deeply trust yourself and your bike.

Beautiful and efficient, riding moto is both the thrill between our legs and the cradle we can re-member ourselves in after two thousand years of patriarchy has fragmented our mothers into commodifiable parts. My obsession with motorcycles is a way to love myself through fear, to take up space where women have historically been denied access. My respect for them is because they're powerful, and with power comes responsibility.

Chopper culture of my 1970s childhood was a statement against mainstream conformity and rigid social norms. So too, will it be our time to ride, not just as a counterculture of Biker Witches, but deeply reconnected multicultural women who choose matriluminous community over individualism and refusal to compete in ways that reinforce patriarchal norms.

*Wheels of Witchcraft* is emergent, like water oases on the blacktop keep appearing up ahead, wherein riding is about the kind of wholeness that is always renewing, always becoming, all the time.

Healing the wounds of motherness isn't just about healing our personal wounds. The archetype of Mother is universal, ancient, vast and abundant—the holy lap we eternally lay our heads in.

Where the wheels meet the road is how we seek Her, and who we meet and honor along the way is how we find Her.

May our two-finger salute continue the tradition of disrupting harmful systems, and give birth to newfound solidarity for healing our motherlines.

Pixie Lighthorse
Author of *The Wound Makes the Medicine*

# Introduction
# Eat, Pray, Motorcycles?

There are certain moments in our lives when we think we've arrived at our destination, only to find ourselves feeling more lost than ever before. It's within these moments that we realize we have no choice but to dig deep and unearth the fragments of our truest selves that have become buried beneath the choices that led us astray.

These pivotal moments look different for each of us. For some, maybe it's the moment we feel in our gut that we married the wrong person. For others, maybe it's the moment we notice the tightness in our throat while accepting a job we know will crush our spirit, or the moment we say yes to a major life decision we silently feel unsure about.

The commonality among all of us who arrive at *that* moment is the seemingly out-of-body experience of realizing that it was with our own shaking hands we signed our souls up for one of the many societal scripts that we, as women, feel obligated to fulfill because we were never told we had any other option.

I've experienced that moment myself.

That's why I feel irrevocably compelled to write these very words to assure you that there is.

I spent my teenage years and early twenties feeling brutally lonely. There were moments of joy, of course, and I made some wonderful memories. Yet, after years of reflection and introspection, I came to understand that many of the major life choices I made during that decade of my life stemmed from a profound wound—one that could only be created by something as earth-shattering as the sudden, tragic, and unexpected loss of my mother.

Feeling strangled by the hands of grief and the harsh reality of death, I was a thirteen-year-old girl who grew up overnight. Gasping for air, I spent a decade of my life trying to survive the pain of losing my best friend by making choices that seemed like the "correct" way to navigate womanhood.

After having just witnessed the sharp decline of my mother's well-being as she was consumed by unaddressed trauma from her childhood and the pain of losing her own mother, my inner child made a promise to herself that her mother's fate would never be her own.

After having just watched the fatal consequences of being entrapped in the vicious cycles of abusive interpersonal relationships, institutional failings, and the alcoholism that can take hold in response to it all, my younger self made a vow to stay on a "straight and narrow" path that would ensure her own survival.

Because I saw what happens when you don't.

So, I made choices. Ones that kept me alive and "safe," but also willing to accept the fact that the life I was building never really felt like my own. Eventually, those choices brought me to my own fateful moment at the age of 23—the night when my obsession with creating a "safe" life left me alone and breathless, crying on my bathroom floor.

As I sat there with my head in my hands, staring at the cold tiles beneath me, I was hit with the hard truth:

I fucking hated my life.

I had become someone I never wanted to be, and I had built an entire reality around avoiding my wounds instead of ever really facing them. I had mistaken comfort for safety, and security for healing, and by refusing to choose myself all those years, my greatest fear had come true:

I was living out my mother's story.

It was right then and there that I understood that what a soul wants and what a wound needs are two very different things. I hit my rock bottom, but within those cries lived a whisper of hope telling me there had to be another way.

There was.

Many of us sign that dotted line knowing full well that whatever script we've just signed ourselves up for completely contradicts who we are at our core, and what we truly desire in our hearts.

Unfortunately, this has been a pattern among women for generations. Whether by force or by choice, we have been living out the generational cycles that teach us—or rather, threaten us—to silence our intuition in order to survive the unrelenting demands of patriarchy.

It's bullshit, I know.

But dare I be so bold as to share a few secrets with you:

*Contracts can be dissolved.*

*Minds are allowed to change.*

*Decisions can be made, unmade, and made again.*

*Our paths can shift at any moment, and we get to choose when.*

Let these secrets be the spells you whisper to yourself as you open the door that leads you to the treasure hunt of the soul. This treasure hunt provides the fertile ground from which you can courageously rebuild and rediscover who you are.

I feel I must warn you that as soon as you open this door, the map of your soul will recalibrate and you'll find yourself idling at a fork in the road with no choice but to take one of two paths.

The first path is safe and predictable. It's well-lit, paved smooth by generations who walked it before you, with clearly marked signs and familiar milestones. Every mile feels already accounted for, as if you're simply following a map drawn by someone else's hand. You know this choice can lead to perfectly good places, maybe even beautiful ones, but something about it will always feel *just* out of alignment deep within your bones.

The second is uncharted. At first, this amount of uncertainty might even feel scary to you, and rightfully so! You know that if you choose this path, you might encounter unexpected speed bumps, steep ledges, blind twists and turns, and any other obstacles that society warns you about the minute you dare to be dangerous.

I am here to tell you that, despite all the disempowering narratives we're fed about women from the moment we're born, you already have the tenacity needed to take this second path.

Whether you're new to the journey of reclaiming your intuitive ways or you've been at it for decades, let this moment serve as a declaration that you are fully capable of using the tools and resources in this book for whatever lies ahead.

With practice, you'll learn how to slow yourself down so that you no longer need to brace for impact with each bump. You'll sharpen your focus on the road so that the ledges surrounding you are nothing but a scenic backdrop, and you'll fully cultivate the ability to navigate the twists and turns so that you can actually enjoy them, leaving only butterflies in your stomach and a smile on your face.

I once found myself at this very junction. I chose the second path, and it led me to a place more fulfilling than I could have ever imagined: a life shaped entirely by my own *sovereign* choosing.

After realizing that my rock bottom was where my own most forgotten riches were buried, I decided to write this book not only as a lifeline for those who might be enduring their own lowest of lows, but also as a grimoire filled with enchanting possibilities for women everywhere to embrace all that an unusual spiritual path can bring.

Possibilities that invite you to take every ride at your own pace, to pull over and savor the sights, to stop and smell the flowers, and to gather with friends under the night sky to rev your engines and howl at the moon.

The rituals that breathe within these pages were born from my own years spent humbly on my knees, weeding out the trauma from my motherline so that magic could finally bloom.

The knowledge within this book was made possible by the teachings of Sadee Whip and Robin Artisson, whose language and insight helped me not only heal from my childhood and reclaim my ancestral roots, but also craft such a unique working system of witchcraft for myself—now ready for you to explore.

Finally, the very reason for this book's existence is because of Her. She who leaves the porch light on for each of us for when we eventually make our way back home to ourselves. Thanks to Her, I've been able to forge a whole new connection with my mother. One that transcends death, time, and dimension. This connection has planted daisies in the hollow spaces within my heart that only a mother's love could ever fill.

It has also provided me with a deeper knowing. The awareness and sincerest of truths that, aside from her love for being a mother, there were two things that gifted me the opportunity to have my mom with me here in this realm for as long as I did—the very things that kept her tethered to life despite her own wounds and our motherline trauma: **motorcycles and witchcraft.**

Getting to know my mother's spirit after her death has unveiled an unconventional and deeply personal path that I am honored to share with you here in this book. Do with it what you will.

Whether you take just one thing or everything away from this experience, my hope is that you make it your own and that it fills your heart with joy, your life with adventure, and your soul with whatever it needs to be as wild as you deserve.

Welcome to the mystical path of the Biker Witch.

# A Pre-Ride Safety Check

Before you swing your leg over your bike and ride off into the unknown, let's take a moment to pause. Just as every responsible rider conducts a thorough pre-ride safety check, this is your opportunity to check in with yourself and consider what you might need to feel safe and steady for the journey ahead.

The themes in this book, especially in this first chapter, are intense. They could stir things that have been long buried, or inherited but not yet felt.

We'll utilize our own T-CLOCS checklist to determine our sense of road-readiness together. I encourage you to visit this space as your starting point every time you open this book to set out again.

### T – Traction

Are you feeling grounded? Is your body calling for water, food, rest, or movement?

Feel your contact with the earth. You are supported.

### C – Controls

Where are you holding tension? Are you gripping too tightly physically or emotionally?

Let your breath soften your grip. You don't have to force this ride.

## L – Lights and Signals

Are you tuned in to your inner signals? What are your emotions or instincts trying to shed a light on?

Check your clarity. Your inner voice has a place here.

## O – Oil and Fluids

What's fueling you today? Are you running on empty?

Let joy, nourishment, and even tears replenish you. You deserve to be full.

## C – Chassis

What are you carrying in your body today? Are there places that feel strained, heavy, or forgotten?

You can adjust. You can shift your weight. You can lean into support.

## S – Stands

Can you pause when you need to? Can you give yourself permission to stop, breathe, and come back later?

Rest is not a detour. It's part of the ride.

While moments of pause to check in with yourself are absolutely essential on this path, having safe people to travel it with is just as important. Those around us can support us when the way forward feels uncertain. They can offer reassurance, witness our vulnerability, and remind us we're never alone.

Within these pages, I've woven together pieces of my own story alongside those of remarkable women from around the world. They are that support for me. Their voices keep me grounded when the going gets rough, and their presence inspires me every day to keep moving forward.

Let me introduce them to you:

**Krista** is a Canadian entrepreneur, stunt rider, mother and female riding advocate based on Vancouver Island, BC. She owns DellaCrew Co.—a lifestyle riding brand and the world's first all-female Harley Davidson stunt team. I first connected with Krista on Instagram and was struck by her fierce determination and her ability to channel vulnerability into a force for connection. She is an invaluable gift to the motorcycle community, and I'm truly honored to know her.

**Serena** is a copywriter, mum, and creative all-round maker, with a cup that's always half full and eyes that look at the world with wonder. Based in the UK, I originally met her online, where we bonded over our shared joy and belief in the beauty, sadness, and magic of the many facets of human nature—not to mention our mutual love of motorcycles! Connecting with her through this project has felt like reuniting with an old friend, and I feel so lucky to have found her again.

**Hex** is a practicing witch and artist, specializing in leatherwork and pieces that honor the native flora and fauna of her homeland in Australia. She has further tapped into her magic through motorcycling, utilizing her bike as both a tool and a conduit for connection to the land and to community. We serendipitously connected on Instagram when I came across her stunning leatherwork. We traded our crafts: one self-guided ritual kit from me for one of her handcrafted belts. That belt became an essential piece adorning my chopper, and our connection blossomed into a lifelong friendship.

**Raegan** is an artist, writer, and television production manager based in Columbus, Georgia, where she lives with her husband and her sweet dog. Her work has been featured in various magazine publications, and you can feel the passion she puts behind her art. We met years ago when we were both living in Washington, and she remains one of my closest thought-partners and confidants. To this day, she's my favorite person to share a love of the beauty that thrives in the Deep South.

**Sabrina** is a wild child from Sacramento, California, who has spent the last 17 years wandering the country, falling in love with cities, national parks, and small towns in her search for a place to call home. Her love for motorcycles began in 2010 while living in Los Angeles, and by 2015, she was fully committed. After moving to San Francisco, she sold both her car and her first bike, a '77 Honda CB200T, to invest in a motorcycle that could take her anywhere. Through motorcycles and the sense of community they foster, Sabrina has found countless adventures and formed lifelong friendships. In 2018, she moved to New Orleans, where she found sisterhood with four other badass women. Together, they ignited the *Moto Maidens*, a docuseries celebrating and showcasing trailblazing women across the United States.

**Francesca** is a practicing witch and passionate creative from Wales who initially crossed my path on Instagram. She had just purchased her first motorbike and ordered a spirit bell from my business to accompany her on her journey. We connected instantly, bound by our shared love for motorcycles and all things witchy, and I'm grateful to have her voice included in these pages.

**Rina** is a doctor from Costa Rica whose life has been shaped by challenges she has faced with unwavering strength and determination. Through those experiences, she came to understand the profound importance of being heard and feeling connected to something greater. That understanding drives her to give back, sharing her knowledge, empathy, and hope with others. When I met Rina online, I immediately sensed something special—a light and a story waiting to be shared. I'm so grateful her story is part of this book.

**Gabrielle** is a master aesthetician based in Seattle, Washington, who finds purpose in helping people feel confident and comfortable in their own skin. Her passion for empowerment extends beyond her treatment room and into the world of motorcycling, where she challenges societal norms and embraces the liberating spirit of the ride. Whether in her work or on the road, Gabrielle is driven by a sincere belief in the strength, independence, and resilience of women. Gabrielle and I instantly became friends when we met in Seattle at a special motorcycle photoshoot for women. We were drawn to each other, knowing we were meant to cross paths in this life.

**Nina** is a software developer from Oslo, Norway, who isn't afraid to plunge into the unknown. Her passion for vintage motorcycles connects her to the roots of motorcycle culture, and she brings that same spirit to everything she creates. Resourceful, creative, and courageous, she faces challenges head-on and channels her energy into making a positive impact in her community. Working with her on this project has been an honor, and her commitment to empowering fellow women riders is truly inspiring. I look forward to the day I can experience firsthand the movement she is building for women and their motorcycles in Norway.

Each of these women brings a truly unique perspective to the world. I can't wait for you to meet them and hear their stories.

꙳

This book is meant to be experienced much like a spell. It's a carefully crafted blend of personal storytelling, rich explorations of identity and culture, soul-stirring philosophies, embodied rituals, and more.

These ingredients will come together to reveal how the worlds of motorcycling and witchcraft, when combined, offer women new ways to reclaim their power and find real healing and belonging within community. Because power, healing, and belonging are inherently political, these first few chapters will guide you through that terrain.

We cannot explore either of these worlds without stepping into the political, as both actively confront the systems that seek to break us. These topics may evoke strong memories, challenge your current perspectives, or require more space to sit with.

That's why I've included Rest Areas at the end of every chapter to encourage you to pull over, stretch, and process. Each Rest Area includes journal prompts, intentional activities, or rituals that invite you to make every minute of this experience your own.

I highly recommend taking the time to thoughtfully engage with these areas as you move through this work. The tools and insights you gain there will become essential for your life as a Biker Witch. They'll also serve as a powerful reflection of how your own learning and integration unfolded during your time reading this book.

Well, sister, it's time for you to hit the road.

Thank you so much for being here.

My heart is full.

# THE ROAD MAP

# The Lay of the Land

I was fortunate to be raised in a family where both motorcycling and witchcraft were integral pieces of our cultural identity. Seeing the bikers pulling into our driveway in their leather cuts felt as casual as watching my favorite cartoons before bedtime. My mother leaving a cup of cream on the hearth as an offering to spirits felt as normal to me as playing with my friends at recess.

For years, these aspects of my day-to-day life felt completely typical. It wasn't until I grew older and my awareness expanded that I began to see just how much they served as portals to new possibilities. I remember sitting with my father in the little shed that stood in our backyard. The space was small—organized, yet wonderfully chaotic—with parts and tools placed exactly where he could find them.

At one point, I paused my coloring and looked over at him. I watched how effortlessly the music from the stereo set a beat he could nod to while turning wrenches. The lyrics seemed to carry meaning straight into his soul, while his hands worked in seamless communication with his brilliant mind, tightening and loosening the bolts that held these beautiful beasts of steel and rubber together.

It was an **ecosystem**. Parts, tools, lyrics, and biker all working together to create and sustain the bikes that gave my parents such meaningful life experiences. Each piece played its part in relation to the others, achieving a kind of harmonious balance. From that moment on, I knew magic was real. You see, what gives life to the reality of magic is **relationship**, and we forge and tend to relationship through **witchcraft**.

I'm sure many women felt drawn to this book because the words "biker" and "witch" together sparked a resonant curiosity. One that stirred something familiar inside them, something they hadn't yet named but instinctively wanted to explore. This curiosity is not without reason. Pop culture has significantly shaped our collective perception of both groups, but especially witches.

Through films, television, and literature, witches are often portrayed either as malevolent entities casting dark and destructive spells, or as seductive figures luring their next victim into a beguiling trap. These portrayals tap into our cultural fears and fascinations around witches, influencing the way we engage with the concept of witchcraft today.

But where do these anxieties and obsessions stem from?

Let's gather at the bridge between the medieval and early modern eras and take in the lay of the land that connects witches with Europe, the Americas, and Africa. From here, history emerges as an overlapping continuum of social, political, and economic forces influencing the world across centuries.

More importantly, we begin to see just how much these forces and witchcraft are intertwined. Ultimately, everything at the root of this entanglement comes down to **power**. Where it comes from, who stole and distorted it, and how those distortions continue to be weaponized to shape the world as we know it.

## The Theft

Our exploration begins in Europe, where the story of power unfolds amid major transformations in land, labor, belief, and authority. Medieval Europe largely operated under a feudal system. Kings and lords controlled territories through force, allegiance, and tradition, while peasants labored in exchange for protection, shelter, and food.

Outside these kingdoms, however, lay the commons.[1] For the working class, the commons were more than just acreage. They were a lifeline that provided essential resources and a rare degree of economic independence for those seeking to supplement their livelihoods or avoid full reliance on feudal labor systems.

By the 14th and 15th centuries, early forms of capitalism began to emerge alongside mercantilism. These systems gradually supplanted the agrarian economy, redefining wealth in terms of money, trade, and capital rather than customary exchange. As a result, merchants, bankers, and traders were able to challenge traditional feudal economic structures, marking a gradual but pivotal transition into the early modern era.

By the 16th century, the enclosure movement gained momentum in England, with similar processes of land privatization occurring in other parts of continental Europe. States and landowners began to fence off the commons, transforming these shared spaces into private property valued for their economic potential.

As large tracts were enclosed and consolidated, many peasants were forcibly displaced, losing access to subsistence resources and being pushed into wage labor under landlords. Such changes severed their longstanding ties to the land, deepened class divisions, and contributed to the growing commodification of the natural world.

Unsurprisingly, the emerging capitalist order was met with widespread resistance. Across Europe, peasants and working-class communities pushed back against the ruling class, only to be met with violent repression.

As capitalism expanded, Europe's ruling class turned outward to secure dominance within a growing global economy by seeking to control trade routes, accumulate wealth, and extend their influence far beyond the continent, thereby setting the stage for

---

1. The commons: shared grounds where local communities grazed animals, foraged for food, gathered firewood, and practiced small-scale farming to support their families.

the so-called Age of Exploration, a term that grossly glosses over the staggering devastation it unleashed.

Contrary to what most textbooks taught in schools, the Americas were not lands "waiting to be discovered." They were already home to thriving Indigenous societies with complex cultures, economies, and intimate connections to the earth. To claim these areas for themselves, European colonizers inflicted calculated violence, spreading deadly diseases, seizing territory through coercion and deception, and committing genocidal atrocities on an unimaginable scale.

As Europeans settled on these stolen lands, they established plantations to produce highly profitable commodities such as sugar, tobacco, and cotton. To sustain these empires, they relied on a new system of labor: the Transatlantic Slave Trade. Millions of Africans were violently taken from their homelands, chained aboard ships, and forced to endure horrific conditions during the Middle Passage.

Those who survived were subjected to relentless violence and systematic dehumanization on plantations. Their stolen labor became the engine driving imperial economies and a central force behind European wealth and expansion, ultimately laying the foundations for a global capitalist system built on colonization and genocide.

Now, what does all of this have to do with witches?

Well, quite a lot.

These empires weren't maintained by violence alone. They also relied on reshaping entire belief systems, social structures, and cultural identities to justify and sustain colonial rule. Accusations of witchcraft became a powerful tool in this effort, used to legitimize forced conversions, erase traditional knowledge systems, and suppress resistance.

The spiritual and healing traditions practiced by Indigenous peoples in the Americas and by enslaved African communities were cast as dangerous, superstitious, or demonic, serving to frame colonization as a moral imperative—an effort to bring "order" and "civilization" to supposedly chaotic or evil cultures.

Women were especially targeted during this process, particularly those who held the role of healers, midwives, herbal doctors, and knowledge keepers. Their roles placed them in direct conflict with colonial authority, and their influence within their communities was perceived as a threat. While colonizers certainly inflicted violence on everyone during this time, women experienced uniquely cruel forms of exploitation.

Enslaved African women faced medical experimentation and control over their reproductive abilities. Often raped by enslavers and overseers and forced to bear children, their bodies were violated and exploited to produce wealth, labor, and future enslaved workers vital to the capitalist system.

Indigenous women endured equally horrific abuses, including forced sterilization meant to erase future Indigenous generations or forced birth of children who were conceived through rape by colonizers, as part of a deliberate effort to "breed out" Indigenous identity over time.

Women were stripped of their personhood and reduced to categories of usefulness, judged solely by their capacity to further the exploits of empire. They were systematically robbed of their identity, autonomy, and inherent connections to both their bodies and ancestral lands as an essential part of the colonial project.

This was not incidental; it was foundational.

**Patriarchy**[2] was built on the subjugation of women, exerting control over both reproduction and production to uphold

---

2. I considered using "colonialism" as the overarching term in this book, but I chose patriarchy because it encompasses multiple systems of oppression, including colonialism, capitalism, white supremacy, and empire. Patriarchy is the "manufactured reality" that makes these systems possible. It organizes power along lines of gender, sexuality, race, and class. No one truly benefits from it outside of the ruling class, yet anyone can uphold it by following its rules, enforcing its expectations, or internalizing its values.

the hierarchy of the ruling class, ensuring their continued accumulation of wealth and domination of resources. It was a violent project orchestrated by colonial men determined to play God, desecrating both flesh and soil in their drive to conquer and commodify nature itself.

## The Distortion

After Europe refined its methods of enforcing patriarchal rule on distant shores, the ruling class brought these strategies back home at a time when local communities were already grappling with crop failures, disease, and widespread social unrest. In this volatile environment, the narrative that witchcraft was behind these local misfortunes spread rapidly, sparking the infamous witch hunts that swept across much of the continent.

Both the Church and the ruling class capitalized on the hysteria. The Church used it to reinforce its authority by suppressing older, localized spiritual practices and encouraging suspicion among neighbors. By labeling witchcraft as heresy, it expanded its influence over social and spiritual life.

Meanwhile, the ruling class exploited the witch hunts to tighten its control. As inequality grew and wealth became more concentrated at the top, accusations of witchcraft redirected public anger toward community members rather than the institutions causing their hardship, allowing those in power to shift blame away from the very systems responsible for the suffering.

Though historical records vary across regions, two patterns consistently emerge: those accused of witchcraft were disproportionately poor or already socially marginalized, and in many areas, the majority of the accused were women.

Feminist scholars and historians have long argued that the witch hunts were part of a broader effort to suppress women's roles as healers, midwives, and custodians of traditional, land-based knowledge. These roles challenged emerging systems of authority that sought to impose rigid hierarchies and prioritize profit over communal well-being.

By targeting women who held knowledge of both the body and the land, those in power sought to eliminate alternative avenues for attaining healing and exercising bodily autonomy. Controlling bodies made it easier to control entire populations, and once populations were under control, the ruling class could more easily seize and exploit the land.

While I believe it's important not to compare the experiences of European women with those of enslaved African and Indigenous women during this time, whose suffering under patriarchal enforcement was distinctly brutal, we can still draw parallels to a broader pattern that is very much relevant for us today:

Imperial systems of domination are often first tested on those most marginalized before being adapted for wider use across society.

Reproductive violence, cultural erasure, and the suppression of ancestral knowledge—tactics used to oppress enslaved African and Indigenous women in the Americas—were later mirrored in Europe in different, but equally intentional ways. The witch trials, while horrible, were only one part of this transformation.

For patriarchy to fully entrench itself, the ruling class needed long-term structures that could reshape society at every level. Over time, community healing traditions were replaced by state-aligned medical systems. What was once passed down through generations of women was now regulated by institutions dominated by colonial men. The body, especially the female body, came to be seen as something to be managed, controlled, and used to serve the interests of the state and the economy.

As European powers consolidated their influence at home and expanded across the globe, patriarchal systems spread with them. They undermined Indigenous sovereignty, dismantled earth-based belief systems, erased spiritual practices tied to the land, and redefined women's roles to fit within colonial and capitalist frameworks.

Community interdependence was replaced by rugged individualism. Relationship gave way to extraction. What emerged was a global system built on disconnection, dependence, and dominance.

You might be wondering what this all has to do with you. Truthfully, it has *everything* to do with you. The atrocities of the early modern era may feel distant, but the systems built to maintain profit, control, and the suppression of women's autonomy remain overwhelmingly embedded in our world.

Colonial imperialism continues to destabilize nations and displace communities in pursuit of power and control. As families flee as refugees and asylum seekers, women and girls face heightened risks of sexual violence and exploitation.[3]

The overturning of Roe v. Wade in the United States exemplifies a broader backlash against bodily autonomy and reproductive justice as part of an ongoing effort to control reproduction, enforce social hierarchies, and deny agency to those deemed less valuable by the system.

The global crisis[4] of missing and murdered Indigenous women and girls underscores the persistent violence of settler colonialism, systemic racism, and misogyny—a direct consequence of centuries of state-sanctioned erasure,

---

3. A pattern evident in the Northern Triangle (El Salvador, Guatemala, Honduras), where historical colonial legacies and contemporary U.S. policies and interventions continue to perpetuate violence, instability, and displacement in the region. An article titled *Women on the Run: First-Hand Accounts of Refugees Fleeing El Salvador, Guatemala, Honduras, and Mexico* stated: "Fleeing is an ordeal in its own right, and for most women, the journey to safety is a journey through hell. After paying exorbitant fees to unscrupulous "coyotes," many women are beaten, raped, and too often killed along the way."

4. In places like Canada and the United States, the legacies of settler expansion, forced displacement, and jurisdictional gaps continue to place Indigenous women at disproportionate risk. Similar dynamics appear in Palestine, where Palestinian women face structural inequality, restricted mobility, and exposure to both state and interpersonal violence under Israeli occupation. Across these contexts, the convergence of colonial land appropriation, erosion of Indigenous sovereignty, and systemic neglect creates a transnational pattern of disappearance, assault, and impunity.

injustice, and structural neglect that leave Indigenous women unprotected.

Environmental collapse—rooted in colonial legacies of resource[5] extraction—remains an ongoing burden. Marginalized communities, particularly in the Global South, bear the heaviest costs of climate change, while women, often traditional stewards of land, water, and communal well-being, navigate increasingly precarious conditions with dwindling resources.

Profit-driven healthcare systems continue to fail women, especially women of color. In the U.S., Black women face disproportionately high maternal mortality rates, a crisis arising from the intersection of racism, sexism, and medical neglect that perpetuates centuries of dehumanization, experimentation, and disregard.

Ideas about labor, productivity, and human worth, shaped by capitalist and colonial values, have entrenched ableism. Women with disabilities, especially mothers, are often shamed for not "doing enough" and simultaneously denied access to necessary support, reflecting a system that values people primarily for economic output and excludes those who don't meet its narrow standards of usefulness.

Trans women, particularly Black trans women, face some of the highest rates of violence, poverty, and systemic neglect, stemming from the compounded effects of racism, misogyny, transphobia, and economic exclusion—forces based in the colonial past and perpetuated by modern institutions.

All of these systems work together to seize power, distorting it from something that once flowed freely through entire

---

5. Overexploited regions such as Sudan and Congo illustrate how colonial legacies continue to shape environmental and social instability. Colonial-era borders and extractive economic systems established by the ruling class perpetuate ongoing conflict, displacement, and ecological degradation. Competition over oil, minerals, and land, driven by corporate interests, fuels cycles of violence. As communities are uprooted and ecosystems deteriorate, women bear disproportionate burdens of violence, insecurity, and resource scarcity.

communities into a force that upholds patriarchy not just as a cultural belief, but as a structural reality.

## The Weapon

Patriarchy was built on and thrives through the strategic weaponization of **fear**. The fear of not having enough, not doing enough, and not being seen as valid, worthy, or deserving. There are few symbols that capture that fear more vividly than the **witch**. Historically, the word "witch" was used as a weapon during the early modern era, but it didn't end there.

The idea of the witch has continued to serve as a tool to control, separate, marginalize, and silence women and other vulnerable groups. Those who defy patriarchal norms are still often branded as dangerous or deviant, facing social exclusion, harassment, or violence. In some parts of the world today, accusations of witchcraft continue to lead to brutal attacks and even killings.

The story of the witch runs like a thread from the era of colonial conquest to modern-day repression, revealing a long-standing battle between systems of control and those who dare to resist them. So, when I say I believe you picked up this book because something stirred in you at the thought of a Biker Witch, I'm not just talking about aesthetics.

Those two words together have probably awakened something ancient within you—a tension between freedom and rebellion on one side, and control and condemnation on the other. Tension lives in both "biker" and "witch," each carrying its own charge of defiance and danger. The friction created in this charge is what makes them so powerful together. Both have been feared, ridiculed, and romanticized, and both have endured.

The figure of the witch lives deep in our collective consciousness, shaped by centuries of oppression, survival, and resistance. For women especially, the weight of this history has been stored in our bodies, minds, and relationships across generations. You may already feel this in your own life, perhaps through stories of colonization impacting your family, or in moments when the words "witch" or "bitch" were used as insults or warnings telling the women in your family to shrink, shut up, or disappear.

The witch also arises during times of collective crisis. Loudly, when something within us is ready to resist and fight back and stand up for each other. Quietly, in the pressure to survive by turning against one another, in the impulse to stay silent, keep our heads down, and feel relief that we're not the ones being burned.

This self-preservation response is not necessarily a reflection of moral character, but a survival tactic ingrained in women under patriarchy. For generations, many women were taught that safety could sometimes be bought at the cost of another woman's pain.

The struggles we face as women right now, both personal and shared, are connected to those who came before us. The colonial systems that once shaped their lives still live on in ours, and the traumas born from those systems haven't vanished. They remain with us, encoded in our biology in ways science is only just beginning to understand.

As Mark Wolynn explains in It Didn't Start With You: How Inherited Family Trauma Shapes Who We Are and How to End the Cycle:

> The most common epigenetic tag is DNA methylation, a process that blocks proteins from attaching to a gene, suppressing its expression. DNA methylation can positively or adversely affect our health by locking "helpful" or "unhelpful" genes in the "off" position. When a stressor or trauma occurs, researchers have observed irregularities in DNA methylation that can be transmitted, along with a predisposition for physical or emotional health challenges, to subsequent generations (30).

This scientific insight offers more than recognition of what we've inherited; it also reveals how our responses to current events stem from survival strategies that are part of a much longer history etched into our bodies. Tracing your own lineage through time will undoubtedly reveal that your ancestors, regardless of their origins, endured violence under patriarchal systems as these systems spread across the globe.

Maintained by a ruling class far smaller than the populations they controlled, these systems relied on intimidation and fear to pressure entire communities into compliance. That compliance wove itself into the nervous systems of our ancestors, leading many to abandon their roots, perpetuate harm, or remain silent while others were accused of witchcraft.

The ancestors who engaged in finger-pointing likely passed down stories about *those* people who practiced these arts, embedding both fear and judgment into the generations that followed.

Similarly, those who were targeted or harmed in these efforts undoubtedly passed down their own stories of survival, often written invisibly in the margins of the man-made rulebook defining what makes a society "safe" and "orderly."

Whatever roles our ancestors held—whether as victims, enablers, resisters, participants, or bystanders—the violence they endured has left a lasting physical and emotional impact on all of us.

## The Return

We each carry a story that began long before we were born. The emotional, physical, and spiritual echoes within you are intertwined with those who walked this earth before you. These echoes will shape how you respond to the words and exercises in the next few chapters ahead. I encourage you to let them.

These moments are precious opportunities to acknowledge the imprints of ancestral trauma still held in your body, where the legacy of witchcraft as danger still lingers in your cells. Over time, your body will begin to sense that you are safe here, and that it is possible to start unraveling what you carry.

This unraveling creates the space you need to explore your generational inheritance in ways that will help you discern what truly belongs to you and what was passed down out of necessity, fear, or pain. Discernment will become a tool to help loosen your grip on survival and transform your ancestors' struggles into sources of strength and guidance.

The entire first section of this book will serve as a roadmap to guide you in this task. It will help you retrace your steps, reflect on where you've been, and gain clarity about where you're going.

Along the way, you'll begin charting your own path, creating memories that are unmistakably yours, and building a tangible record of the pivotal moments when you began defining your life as a witch on your own terms, free from the burdens passed down with the label.

Our roadmap will offer the guidance you need to stay the course, but the journey itself is not necessarily straightforward. The path of the Biker Witch is not linear or predictable. It bends, spirals, and may lead you down unfamiliar roads.

However, within this wildness lies the chance to imagine a life where your worth is no longer measured by how well you comply with systems never meant to protect you, but instead by your courage to reclaim what was once stolen, dismantle what was built to harm, and carry forward a different truth.

You might encounter some roadblocks—moments when the weight of current events and inherited pain feels too heavy to bear, leading you to wonder, "What's even the point?" But that question is an important part of the work.

When we connect the pieces of our shared histories, we see that present pain and past injustice are not isolated events or reflections of personal failure, but parts of a larger, ongoing system that has been manufactured to divide, suppress, and disconnect us.

By recognizing this, we uncover the intersectionality of our wounds and the collective burdens we carry under patriarchy, and we let ourselves believe that **what has been built can also be broken.**

The witchcraft we call upon here to assist us in this revolutionary breaking is ancient and embodied. It lives in our blood and in the memory of our ancestors—especially our foremothers—whose lives and struggles we will tend to with intention by meeting their pain with compassion.

This craft will support us as we face our own wounds, heal the ancestral trauma carried through our lineages, and clear the way for our magic to flow freely once more.

It will also help us restore our capacity to care for one another, both within our immediate communities and across a global sisterhood of women riding alongside us.

Because even in our individuality, we were never meant to ride through this life alone.

Together, we'll find who we are beneath the conditioning and beyond the fear, making the path of the Biker Witch ultimately one of riding, remembering, and returning.

A **ride** that reconnects us to our bodies, our instincts, and the power that was always meant to be ours.

A ritual of **remembering** who we were long before harmful systems told us who we should be.

A **return** to a life of belonging, beyond the bounds of patriarchy.

# Rest Area #1

Welcome to your first Rest Area. This is a space to connect with what lives inside you and all that longs to be seen. Here, you'll find questions to ponder and answer in your journal. I invite you to respond in ways that reflect where and who you are right now. There are no wrong answers, only gentle markers to look back on and see how much you've evolved throughout this journey.

You'll also be guided in crafting an empowering sigil to take with you on the road. The fear of witchcraft runs deep within our cells, whether we come from the lineages of the accused or the accusers, and building embodied safety around it is essential. Creating your own personal sigil sends a clear message to your nervous system that you are safe to practice this craft and be who you truly are in this world.

## Tools You'll Need

- A journal

- A writing utensil

- Separate piece(s) of drawing paper for sigil making

1. WHAT HAS THE WORD "WITCH" SYMBOLIZED FOR YOU THROUGHOUT YOUR LIFE?

2. WHAT DO YOU KNOW ABOUT YOUR ANCESTORS? TAKE A MOMENT TO JOT DOWN ANYTHING THAT COMES TO MIND.

3. WHERE IN THE WORLD ARE YOUR ANCESTORS FROM? IF YOU'RE NOT SURE, MAKE A NOTE TO EXPLORE THIS FURTHER BEFORE THE NEXT CHAPTER'S REST AREA.

4. HOW HAS THE HISTORY OF COLONIZATION SHAPED YOUR UNDERSTANDING OF POWER, CONTROL, AND EXPLOITATION TODAY?

5. IN WHAT WAYS DO YOU SEE THE HISTORICAL SCAPEGOATING OF MARGINALIZED GROUPS AS "WITCHES" REFLECTED IN HOW CERTAIN COMMUNITIES ARE TREATED NOW?

6. CAN YOU IDENTIFY ANY PARTS OF YOUR ANCESTRY AFFECTED BY COLONIZATION? HOW HAS THAT INFLUENCED YOUR CURRENT WORLDVIEW?

7. HOW DOES THE IDEA OF ANCESTRAL TRAUMA RESONATE WITH YOU? DO YOU NOTICE PATTERNS OF TRAUMA PASSED DOWN IN YOUR FAMILY?

8. HOW DO YOU EXPERIENCE OR RECOGNIZE THE IMPACT OF PATRIARCHY IN YOUR OWN LIFE?

9. WHAT DOES RECLAIMING THE FIGURE OF THE WITCH MEAN TO YOU PERSONALLY?

10. WHAT DOES RECLAIMING YOUR POWER LOOK LIKE IN THE CONTEXT OF YOUR PERSONAL HISTORY AND IDENTITY?

## Create Your Personal Sigil

### 1. Write Your Intention

Start by writing a clear, loving intention for this path of reclamation that reassures your nervous system you are safe to be yourself now.

This intention should be written as a positive affirmation. It could be something like:

*I AM ROOTED IN MY POWER.*
*I TRUST MY MAGIC.*
*I AM SAFE TO BE WHO I AM.*

Keep it simple, honest, and true to what you need.

### 2. Find Your Core Letters

Write your phrase in all capital letters. Then, remove all vowels (A, E, I, O, U) and remove any repeated consonants, keeping only one of each letter.

For example, with the phrase:

*I AM ROOTED IN MY POWER.*

Remove vowels A, E, I, O and repeated consonants, leaving only one M, R, T, D, N, Y, P, and W.

### 3. Shape Your Sigil

With the remaining letters, begin to draw.

Distort or abstract the letters, overlaying or intertwining them until you come up with a shape that feels powerful or resonant in your body.

Adorn your sigil with additional lines, curves, dots, or symbols that feel meaningful.

Your sigil should feel uniquely yours, something that only you would be able to read or recognize.

*EXAMPLE:*

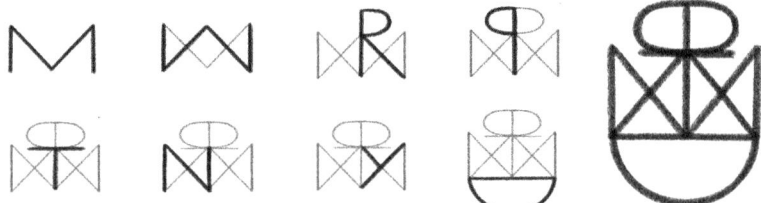

## 4. Empower Your Sigil

Hold your sigil in your hands or place it in front of you.

Take a moment to recall the intention behind the sigil.

Use your breath to empower it.

Inhale deeply.

Exhale slowly through your mouth, directing your breath into the sigil to breathe life into it.

Your sigil is now alive, charged, and empowered.

## 5. Keep It Close

Keep your sigil close so it can signal to your nervous system that it's safe to embrace your life as a witch.

You might stitch it into your leathers, paint it on your gas tank, tattoo it on your body, tuck it into your journal, or place it on your altar.

Every time you see it, let it anchor you back into your intention and the truth that your magic is real, your power is yours, and you are free to shine.

# Find Your Footing

Finding your footing on a spiritual path is a lot like riding a motorcycle along a gravel road. It can feel unsteady, a bit bumpy, and every move requires a delicate balance. No matter how much coaching you receive from others, the journey is ultimately yours to navigate. It's your patience, your determination, and your trust in yourself that will carry you toward steadier ground.

There are countless voices out there that will tell you how to live as a witch—how to manifest your greatest desires or ascend from this world so you no longer have to be a part of it. Even a simple Google search can quickly overwhelm you with unsolicited advice and endless sales pitches promising to enhance your practice.

Take comfort in the fact that the witchcraft explored here emerges from a worldview far older than the word itself. We'll work from these ancient roots not to bypass history or the many ways you may have already engaged with magic in your life, but to offer everyone the chance to start from a place that existed long before our collective lens became clouded by trends or the pressure to acquire expensive ritual wares.

I invite you to lower the volume on everything you've been told about witchcraft. Better yet, turn it off completely. Let's revisit a few hints I shared in the last chapter, specifically the notes about power. We explored how patriarchy shapes the world today and acknowledged that colonial men built it, but now it's time to uncover *where* they found the power to do so.

Many generations ago, your ancestors shared a special relationship with the lands they called home. They moved in rhythm with the seasons, understood the migration patterns of animals, the growth of plants, and the elements that shaped their environment.

This bond reached far beyond what could be seen with the eyes or felt with a touch. It was an intimate connection with the entire landscape, one that imparted the wisdom that everything on Earth is alive and imbued with spirit.

This worldview, what we now call **animism**, blurs the lines our modern world draws between living and non-living, sacred and mundane. It re-enchants us to see life and spirit in all things, grounding us in a broader spiritual ecosystem where all beings exist and interact within a web of relationship.

Within this web, the spirits of all beings—humans, trees, plants, rivers, mountains, stones, lakes, meadows, animals, and even objects made by human hands—are intimately interconnected, interdependent, and co-creative.

Many cultures also recognize an Unseen[1] dimension to this web, where ancestral spirits, the spirits of the dead, non-human spirits, and other mysterious forces believed to shape and influence the world participate in this ecosystem.

What may seem lifeless to many today carries its own agency from an animistic perspective. A motorcycle, for example, is not just a machine to be bought and owned. It is a spirited companion, crafted by human hands—whether entirely or modified with our own tools—that we bond with and care for, and which, in turn, carries us across both physical and spiritual landscapes.

---

1. The ways these beings are understood and honored differ according to each culture's landscapes, histories, and ancestral practices. The Biker Witch path is an extension of my own practice, honoring an Unseen dimension as I experience and interpret it, forming the foundation for ancestor veneration. As you explore your own ancestral lens on the spirit world, you can adapt this path in ways that feel authentic and true for you.

Similarly, the candles, oils, crystals, and tools we work with in our spells are not just things to be used and discarded; they are allies, each with their own indwelling spirit with whom we collaborate.

For most of human history, animism was a universal way of understanding the world. While the ways humans communed with spirits varied across traditions, they all engaged with them as a natural part of life.

These interactions weren't for personal or communal benefit alone; they also reflected a deeper understanding of power. Our ancestors understood power as the **vital force within all things**.

They also understood that power wasn't something to be controlled or exploited, but something to be honored, respected, and restored each time it was drawn upon.

Whenever they asked spirits for support with their human lives, they made offerings to nourish them. When the spirits were nourished, they would offer insight and guidance in return, completing the reciprocal exchange.

The connections between humans and their spirit kin were not transactional, but relational. They were grounded in **right relationship**[2] and upheld through a shared responsibility to sustain the ecological balance of power.

## Reclamation

As patriarchy spread across the world, the power held and sustained within these relationships was viewed as a threat to systems that rely so heavily on disconnection.

Humans were violently separated from their spirit relationships. The ways our ancestors once related to the beings around them were suppressed, outlawed, or colonized and forcibly reshaped

---

2. Right Relationship: the state of being in **harmonious and reciprocal** connection with other beings and the organic processes and cycles that shape life itself.

to fit within the rigid frameworks of hierarchical, monotheistic ideologies.

In their place, patriarchal systems found ways to siphon power away from entire communities, concentrating it into the hands of the ruling class and compelling humans to participate in and rely on the systems they had created instead.

Animism continues to live on in certain parts of the world, where Indigenous peoples have managed to safeguard these belief systems and pass them down through the generations. Unfortunately, for much of the rest of humanity, this way of life has been lost. The histories that once connected us to spirits have been buried, silenced, or rebranded beyond recognition.

To know what once was, and what could have been, is its own kind of grief. May it bring you comfort to know that despite every effort to suppress it, this magic still lives within you. Just as your body carries the cellular memories of the trauma your ancestors endured, it also holds their memories of a connected and powerful life before patriarchy.

Colonizers may have weaponized the word "witch" for their own ends, but that word has always been *ours*. The fact that you've made it this far suggests you know this to be true. Although our ancestors likely never used the term "witch" to identify themselves, we'll honor their timeless wisdom by reclaiming the word and transmuting it from a weapon once used against them into a tool to carry that wisdom forward.

It's not my place to define what it means to be a witch for everyone, as each journey is personal and unique. However, on the path of the Biker Witch, a witch is:

**Someone who utilizes *the art of relationship* to connect with spirits and allows themselves to be transformed by the insight and guidance they receive.**

When I first began writing this book, I often returned to Robin Artisson's definition of what it means to be Witched: "touched by Otherworldly forces and given special benefits, powers, knowledge, insights, abilities, or extraordinary help of some kind, to accomplish something in the human world that they would not otherwise have been able to accomplish" (*The Clovenstone Workings*, p. 12).

There's a quiet significance in this subtle mention of the human world, a detail worth pausing over. Later, we'll delve deeper into our place as witches in our human communities. For now, consider this: the spirits we work with as witches offer what they deem necessary for us to carry back to others among us.

Contrary to what you may currently believe, everything you need to practice this art already lives within you. It is your birthright to connect with the world in this way. It's already a part of who you are. As Robin Artisson explains in his book *The Clovenstone Workings: A Manual of Early Modern Witchcraft*:

> Witchcraft, though it certainly appealed to stranger souls who lived within human communities, was always a form of extraordinary relationship or engagement that was largely *sought out* by the people who would become Witches. A meeting (or meetings) with spirit-persons of some power or influence within the local landscape, the spirits of the dead, or an encounter with even more mysterious spirits of greater power—and the initiatory transformations bestowed upon a man or woman by those spirits in those meetings—was the gateway into historical Witchcraft (11).

At its heart, witchcraft has always been about the art of engaging in reverent, reciprocal relationships with spirits. I call these relationships an art because that's precisely what they are.

They require our active participation, creativity, and steady commitment to the ongoing work of bringing something meaningful into being. Through these connections something new always emerges—a fresh understanding, a healing insight, or a deepened trust.

Spirits have always been a part of our world, not necessarily *waiting* to be remembered but patiently holding steady, ready for the moment when we finally embrace our responsibility to repair our relationship with them.

It is humans who have lost touch with the spirits, not the other way around, and so it becomes our sacred duty to reclaim what has long been forgotten or ignored. Those who dare to devote themselves to a path of relationship with spirits are the ones who truly step into their life as a witch.

Not just in name, but in action.

Your life as a witch will bring many truths, mysteries, and moments of great amusement. But be warned: it will also demand that you swim in deeper waters of accountability, integrity, and the courage to embody both. This responsibility is one that the spirits themselves place upon us.

As you move through this work, you will be challenged. You'll be pushed over and pulled under, compelled to surrender to a current that turns you inward and forces you to confront the many ways your conditioning under harmful systems has kept you closed off to the spirit world.

You will also have to honestly acknowledge where you too have benefited from patriarchy and commit to the lifelong work of dismantling it within yourself and beyond. Though this level of accountability may feel unsettling, I promise the life it opens for us is so incredible that even the challenges become part of what makes this work truly worthwhile.

You are being pulled back to these Old Ways of magic not only to find your footing in an animistic worldview and reconnect with the spirits, but also to shake up your reality just enough to collapse the colonial idea that time is linear. It wasn't time that severed our connection to the world around us, but the conditioning that taught us to look away.

That same conditioning appears when we're told that events throughout history are too distant to matter. People often say, "It was so long ago, why care?"

But patriarchy isn't behind us. It's here. It breathes through the systems that govern our lives, pulses through our bodies, and echoes through our lineages. The trauma it generates isn't history. It lives in us, just as it lived in our ancestors. The wounds, and the structures that caused them, have never truly healed or ended. They are a continuum.

When we begin to understand time not as linear but as spiral, as fluid, as something alive and responsive, we step into a greater reality where the past, present, and future are intertwined. We learn to engage the past, show up fully in the now, and open new pathways toward the future all at once.

Within that non-linear reality, we also release the pressure to be perfect. We drop the illusion that this work is something to finish in a single lifetime. The goal is liberation, but not only our own. We are part of a long lineage of resistance. What we do today becomes part of a future we may never see, but still believe in.

Each return to a lesson, a ritual, or a memory is not a step backward but a deepening. Every act of care, clarity, and courage becomes part of the ongoing work of reclaiming our power.

This path is not a straight road to resolution but a return to what matters, again and again, with new eyes and a deeper layer of understanding until we make our way back to a life where our relationships with spirits feel as natural as the warmth of the sun on our skin or the dirt beneath our feet.

When we are able to feel life as it truly is, not as what we've been forced to believe it should be, we also come to see that power has always been within our reach through the flesh, bone, root, and soil to which we've always belonged, rather than through the systems that withhold it.

We begin to experience freedom in its most raw and embodied sense, instead of the hollow promise of freedom sold to us by the colonial empire—the kind that lives in integrity, intuition, and truth and reshapes the world within us as much as the world around us.

## Attunement

As witches, our magic will contribute to the dismantling of oppressive systems, and it will also fill our own lives with more possibility. Our healing will become part of the world's healing. Our remembering will become part of the world's remembering.

We'll restore what has long been extracted from us and heal the continuum of life itself by reclaiming our rightful place within it and returning power to the roots from which it was taken.

If this sounds like a daunting task, remember that patriarchy has worked hard to destroy our connections to the spirits for a reason. Their wisdom and strength far surpass that of the structures we seek to shatter.

So, where do we go from here? How do we take our first step into the rest of our lives as witches on this path?

We begin by attuning ourselves to the ecosystems we already inhabit, letting ourselves be guided by curiosity and a relentless desire to tend to what lives within them. Attunement invites us to look closely, listen fully, and engage with the stories, memories, and relationships that shape these spaces.

This practice strengthens our ability to notice where wounds linger and where repair is possible. Deepening into such a level of presence also helps us feel the difference between false connection and true kinship.

What we discover within that difference begins to reshape us, integrating into both our relational understanding and our witchcraft practice.

Curiosity, presence, attunement, and integration then become the essential skills we carry into our spirit relationships. Before I send you off to go your own way into those workings, we'll come together on common ground in the living, breathing ecosystem of motorcycling. We are Biker Witches, after all.

Together, we'll nurture the skills of paying attention and noticing. I'll guide you in this. Through that, we'll cultivate something healing, based in the knowledge of where we come from and who we are today.

We'll also practice turning inward, examining how we've been shaped by the culture we love and how our own conditioning under patriarchy shapes it in return.

Motorcycling, as both a lived experience and a vibrant culture, offers fertile ground for this work. It teaches us how to move with, ride alongside, and relate deeply to the world.

Where the path of the witch meets the roar of the road, we find the mystical ground on which to cultivate the skills that will carry us further into the mystery.

# Rest Area #2

You've just found your footing in the Old Ways of magic and begun reclaiming a spiral sense of time. Now it's time to step fully into that spiral and listen to what it carries. At this Rest Area, you'll reconnect with the sacred days, seasons, and celebrations of your ancestors. Your people might come from many places and traditions, and you are welcome to draw from any part of your lineage.

There is no need to have all the answers. This practice is open to everyone. Whether you come from a lineage with intact rituals or are sensing ancestral memory for the first time, your entry point is valid here. I encourage you to explore books, songs, foods, and folkloric stories connected to your ancestral regions, as these are all excellent gateways into ancestral reclamation.

You will also honor the rhythms that shape your life today. These may be personal cycles you move through intuitively, milestones marked by joy or grief, or moments your soul recognizes as holy. The connections you draw between your life and your ancestors will provide keen insight into the continuum of tradition, magic, and intuitive connection to the earth.

## Tools You'll Need

- A journal

- A writing utensil

- 3 pieces of drawing paper

### Listening to Your Ancestors' Rhythms

#### Agricultural, Seasonal, and Celestial Events

- What natural events marked the changing seasons where your ancestors lived? *Examples might include solstices, equinoxes, planting seasons, or harvest festivals.*

- How did shifts in weather and daylight shape rituals, celebrations, and community life?

- How did animal behaviors or other seasonal changes influence the timing or nature of these events?

- How did these events and rituals shape the way your people connected within their communities? Did your ancestors move through these times with quiet reflection, or did they express their connection loudly through song and dance?

#### Rites of Passage and Life Cycles

- Were there any rites connected to the cycles of life (birth, coming of age, marriage, death)?

- What stories or practices were passed down around these thresholds?

#### Natural Thresholds and Sacred Spaces

- If your ancestral history is unclear or unknown, what natural seasonal markers or rituals feel especially meaningful or sacred to you personally?

- How do your body, mind, and spirit respond when you experience these moments?

- What sensations, emotions, or insights arise as you connect with these natural rhythms?

**Giving Form to Rhythm**

**1. Create Your Ancestral Seasonal Wheel**

Draw a large circle divided into four parts for the seasons: spring, summer, fall, and winter.

Within each quadrant, place your findings for your ancestors' rhythms as markers along the wheel. Use words, symbols, colors, or images that reflect how your ancestors may have experienced each season.

You are welcome to add additional lines or sections if you want to make your wheel more specific. Many wheels of the year include eight segments to reflect solstices, equinoxes, and cross-quarter days. You can adapt the design in any way you see fit.

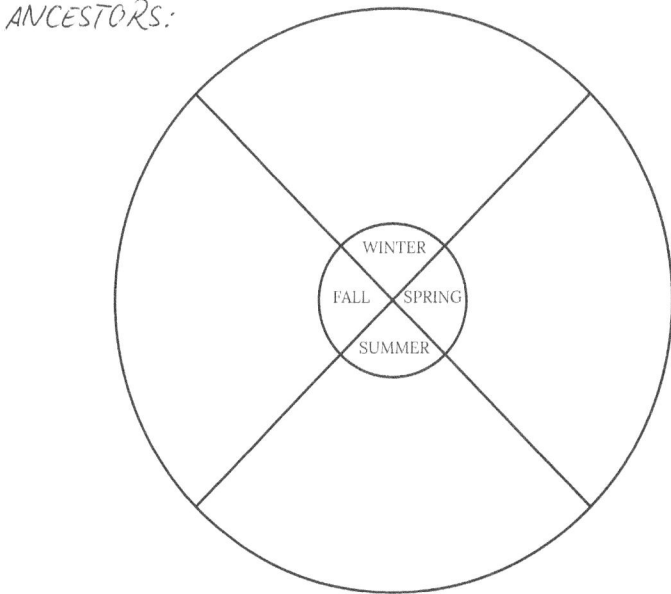

ANCESTORS:

WINTER

FALL   SPRING

SUMMER

**Note:** Some ancestral calendars recognized only two primary seasons, such as summer and winter, or measured time through lunar cycles, wet and dry phases, or other rhythms specific to their culture or region. Feel free to make it your own based on what information feels most relevant to you and your ancestors.

## 2. Create Your Personal Seasonal Wheel

On your second piece of paper, draw the same circle divided into your chosen number of segments.

Use this space to map out your own life rhythms as they align with the seasons where you live.

Add personal milestones, celebrations, phases of growth or rest, and inner changes that show how you move through each season.

This wheel serves as both a personal calendar and a reflection of your embodied seasonal rhythm in your current environment and life.

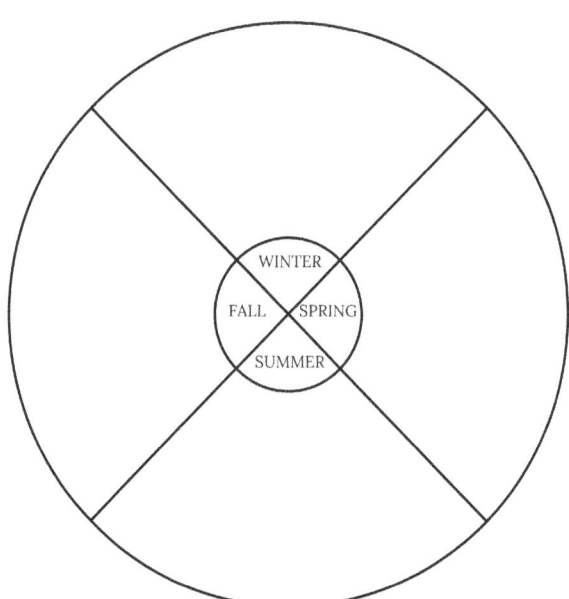

## 3. Weave Past, Present, and Future

Now, bring your ancestral and personal wheels together. Place them side by side and compare them season by season. Notice the similarities and what feels different.

## 4. Reflect On What Emerges

- What themes appear in both wheels?

- Are there values, stories, or rituals that carry through time?

- What practices could bridge your ancestral roots with your current rhythms and rituals?

## 5. Combine Both Wheels

On your third piece of paper, combine both wheels into one final illustration. This combined wheel offers insight into the spiral nature of time, where the past, present, and future intertwine.

As your connection to the land, the seasons, and your lineage deepens, this wheel will continue to evolve with you.

Keep it somewhere visible, perhaps by your altar or workspace, so you can return to it and add to it as your relationship with ritual and rhythm expands.

What you have created here will serve as a foundation for future explorations into timing, embodiment, ancestral relationship, and seasonal alignment.

# A Remedy for the Road

Adrenaline, fire, and fuel all come together in the world of motorcycling to create a lifestyle steeped in intensity and movement. This lifestyle draws people from all walks of life searching for freedom, but like every other place where freedom exists, patriarchy has slowly encroached, suffocating what was once wild and alive.

We'll begin our exploration of this ecosystem by reclaiming our roles as healers within the community. Like tending a witch's herb garden, healing requires vigilance. When invasive growth threatens to overtake the land and stifle its potential, it becomes our responsibility to restore the balance.

Together, we'll address the wounds that patriarchy has inflicted on this ecosystem, clearing away harm with our shared love for this realm and transforming what remains into a potent remedy that is both restorative and inherently revolutionary.

As my favorite revolutionary leader, Fred Hampton, once said, "A lot of people get the word revolution mixed up, and they think revolution's a bad word. Revolution is nothing but like having a sore on your body, and then you put something on that sore to cure that infection." In this spirit, we will heal and nurture this world back to vitality and wholeness.

Imagine yourself as a forager moving through this vast landscape, gathering the wisdom, lessons, and strength needed to carefully blend potential into a remedy in your mortar and pestle. This medicine will do more than heal the community as it exists today.

It will also expand our capacity to imagine and shape a future where the spirit of motorcycle culture can truly thrive again, creating space for regeneration and allowing what has long been suppressed to finally flourish.

Anyone who rides a motorcycle today stands on the shoulders of those who dared to pioneer alternative ways of navigating the world. Courageous souls from past generations handed down keys to the wisdom we'll need for the road ahead, and now, with those keys in our own hands, we honor their journeys by turning their wisdom into possibility for ourselves and for those yet to come.

We'll begin gathering the ingredients for our remedy by applying an animistic lens to the landscape we move through. Each ingredient carries a spirit with which we'll collaborate, and we approach them with respect in our hearts and gratitude ready to be offered.

## Nuance

Our remedy begins with a base ingredient: **nuance**. Nuance, our wise companion, helps create a cohesive mixture strong enough to challenge and counter the societal stereotypes and assumptions often projected onto bikers.

One symptom of living in a patriarchal world is the inability to hold multiple truths at once, which leads us into binary thinking traps that divide us rather than unite us. Cultivating space in your mind for nuance makes you more skillful when handling the inevitably tough conversations that come with being a part of this world.

For instance, many people today view bikers as either good or bad. However, a more nuanced perspective reveals that, like any group of individuals, bikers are not defined by a single moral stance. Within this community lies a diverse range of people, each with their own unique beliefs, values, and actions. Passing judgment based solely on association with this group oversimplifies their complexity.

Similarly, when people say motorcycles are dangerous, we can challenge this singular way of thinking by reframing it. Motorcycles, like any other spirited being, have their own agency. They are not inherently safe or dangerous. Their safety depends on how they are engaged with, the intentions of the person interacting with them, and the actions of the community surrounding them.

Nuance will not only support us in conversation, but it will also allow us to now examine history from multiple angles and perspectives. The world of motorcycling is rich with history, and if I were to write about every single moment that informs our understanding of the culture today, there would be no space for any other chapters in this book.

Instead, we can work with nuance to explore a few key overlapping truths that inform us simultaneously:

1. Motorcycle culture in the United States thrives today in large part because of veterans who sought connection and belonging after returning home from war.

2. While their positionalities were different, the same systems built by the ruling class to colonize and control the world long ago continue to abandon many of the people they send to fight in their name.

3. Historically, motorcycle culture became a refuge for those marginalized by society—a space where healing, freedom, and solidarity could take root outside the systems that treated them as disposable.

After World War II, American veterans returned to a society that was completely unrecognizable. In her article titled *Readjustment & Postwar Life*, Kathleen Frydl expresses the many ways in which society changed while these soldiers were away at war:

Wartime changes transformed the home front, even behind the closed doors of family life. Six million women entered the paid labor force for the first time during the war, joining the roughly 13 million already working for wages. These new entrants to the wage labor market were encouraged to return to housework once the war was over, an expectation that did not always sit comfortably with those asked to fulfill it. A surge in marriages at the start of war was followed by a spike in divorces immediately after it. Housing shortages were pervasive, especially in areas of the defense industry. A younger, unmarried veteran returning home could easily find himself living with his parents for longer than anticipated; an older married one might return to a wife who had forged a new sense of independence while he was gone. These and many other potential points of strain led author Maxwell Droke to advise veterans that their transition to civilian life would be easier 'were it not for two things: your family and friends.'

The emotional turmoil many veterans carried from their wartime experiences was compounded by these challenges of reconnecting with loved ones and adjusting to the societal changes that occurred during their absence. Lacking adequate resources and support for reintegration, many veterans faced isolation and alienation. The camaraderie they had known in the military was difficult to replicate, leaving them longing for the bonds they once had.

To further complicate things, many veterans began to critically reflect on the motives behind war, recognizing its ties to the ruling class's ongoing pursuit of power, resource extraction, and economic gain. This skepticism is echoed in the words of Navy Commander and combat veteran Harvey L. Thorstad, who remarked, "War is for the corporate elite and their exploitation of other countries. Look beyond the noble propaganda of our politicians to the real motives for war" (Hill).

By the end of World War II, the U.S. had emerged as a global economic power, producing a significant share of the world's goods. These shifts sparked widespread discussions about the war's complex motivations, leading many veterans to wrestle internally with the supposed reasons for the United States' involvement, the hidden realities beneath them, and how those motives shaped their own lives.

Alone and deeply traumatized, veterans came together and found the courage to take healing into their own hands. Drawing on the mechanical skills they had developed during their time in service, they gathered in garages and backyards to work on motorcycles.

This marked a pivotal shift in motorcycle culture. While motorcycles had already existed in the United States for decades, post-World War II America saw the culture evolve into a vital outlet for veterans seeking support from others who could not only share their pain, but also held the desire to reclaim their identities in a society that had isolated and exploited them.

Motorcycle culture provided a sense of purpose and community. A space where veterans could find solidarity with those who understood the complexity of their experiences. Embracing nuance within this space became a tool for survival. For many, surviving war alongside fellow servicemen was a profound source of pride. Yet it was equally valid, and necessary, to wrestle with conflicted feelings about the motives that led them there and the far-reaching consequences that followed.

Beyond this, veterans discovered what it could look like to take ownership of their own healing journeys in the absence of government support. Despite promises made through programs like the GI Bill, systemic barriers—including racial discrimination, bureaucratic delays, and a lack of psychological care—often left them to navigate recovery alone.

**Motorcycles became a way to cultivate community, carve pathways toward healing, and reimagine masculinity and camaraderie within the ruins of patriarchy.**

Through motorcycling, veterans found not only recovery but inspiration. They used their skills to build bikes, improve their lives, and reimagine a world beyond greed and the seemingly misleading narratives pushed by the United States government.

In this newfound freedom, they created a radical culture of brotherhood that led to the rise of motorcycle clubs across the nation. Though incredible, their defiance of institutional norms also reflected a troubling historical pattern explored earlier in this book:

**Groups that challenge harmful systems by embracing alternative ways of living, especially those outside the confines of patriarchy, are often demonized and vilified.**

Whether through motorcycle subcultures or earth-based spiritual practices, these outlets challenge the structures that uphold the ruling class. Because of this, they often face hysteria and persecution, revealing both the ruling class's desperate need for control and society's resistance to anything that threatens the status quo.

A striking example of this hysteria occurred in 1947, when approximately 4,000 riders gathered in Hollister, California, for the Gypsy Tour, a Fourth of July ride and rally organized by the American Motorcyclist Association (AMA). While the event was undeniably rowdy, with street racing, drunken brawls, and about 50 arrests, it was the media's portrayal—especially an article in *Life Magazine*—that sparked widespread panic. Instead of showing the rally as a spirited celebration of motorcycle culture that got a little out of hand, the press labeled it a "riot," casting bikers as reckless marauders who had taken over the town.

This sensationalized story not only deepened the marginalization of those who found refuge and meaning in the culture, but also cemented the harsh stereotypes that continue to shadow bikers today.

The fear-mongering in that *Life Magazine* article reveals a powerful throughline to the past: the same deliberate use of fear that once subjugated and scapegoated people during the early modern era still operates today, now aimed at subcultures like motorcycling.

The uncomfortable truth we must confront is that all of us have, at some point, fallen into this fear trap. As we navigate our lives as both bikers and witches, we are also called to examine how we may have unknowingly upheld or contributed to these fears.

This might look like gatekeeping our community out of fear of not being accepted, treating others as competition out of fear of being overlooked, speaking poorly of others out of fear of not being seen as valid, or withholding knowledge and resources out of fear of being depleted or replaced.

These patterns don't emerge in isolation. There is responsibility here. Until we name and dismantle the fears deliberately crafted by those who profit from our disconnection, the cycles of division and hysteria will persist.

Division driven by fear is patriarchy's greatest weapon. The ruling class thrives on fractured communities and poisoned solidarity, ensuring our energy is spent battling one another instead of confronting the systems that truly oppress us.

Becoming a Biker Witch is a bold act of reclamation, but it also means acknowledging both the struggles and the resilience of those who came before us—those who embraced alternative paths and were punished for it.

## Hope

To move forward, we must take full responsibility for breaking harmful cycles and co-creating the kind of community that heals rather than harms. This is why our revolutionary remedy includes a vital second ingredient: **hope**.

While the trauma and othering experienced within this community are undeniably real, we must be careful not to linger too long in the pain. If we stay fixated on the wound, we risk losing sight of what's possible. Without hope, we may never find the inspiration or the perspective we need to fight for something so rewarding.

That's why learning from the bold souls who've embraced motorcycling as resistance is so important. Their refusal to conform to the status quo offers hope for the road ahead. Though we owe much to the brave servicemen who revealed motorcycling as an antidote to patriarchy's pressures, we deepen that understanding by uncovering the often-untold stories of the women who have ridden alongside them all along:

Trailblazers like Della Crewe, a pioneering long-distance motorcyclist, defied both physical and social limitations when she set out on a cross-country journey from Waco, Texas, to New York City in 1914.

Bessie Stringfield, known as the "Motorcycle Queen of Miami," broke through racial and gender barriers in the 1930s and 1940s as the first Black woman to ride solo across the United States, courageously navigating a segregated America on two wheels.

Dorothy "Dot" Robinson founded the Motor Maids in 1940, establishing one of the first women's motorcycle organizations in North America. She also proved herself a fierce competitor in endurance races, challenging the widespread belief that motorcycling belonged to men.

These women, and countless others like them, have boldly resisted systems that sought to confine them. They inspire us to reclaim the road as a space of liberation for ourselves. Learning about their stories helps us redefine what's possible for women in patriarchal world.

## Discernment

By having the audacity to be who they are, bikers have always held up a mirror to the world around them. That mirror reflects how patriarchy has cultivated a deep soul-sickness that still affects us today. It brings into focus the barriers that prevent us from truly understanding and supporting one another, while also offering a vision for how we might begin to heal.

The motorcycling community—once rooted in connection, mutual care, and shared resistance—can be reclaimed and rebuilt on those very foundations. Here, we arrive at the third and final ingredient for our revolutionary remedy: **discernment**. Discernment between the wounds and the medicine in this world is what will carry us forward on our path.

Discernment isn't always gentle work. Though it is an ingredient in our overall remedy, it is also a standalone spirit we must remain in constant communication with. Sometimes, it reveals that no remedy is possible—no nuance to be found, no hope to hold—within a given space, relationship, or structure.

In those moments, we must remember that walking away, grieving, or refusing to pour energy into something completely broken is not failure. It is wisdom, survival, and love directed inward.

Each day offers a new opportunity to notice when the voice of patriarchy is speaking through old wounds or when the medicine of genuine connection is guiding us toward something more whole. When discernment is possible, we are invited into daily relationship and practice with it. This is especially true in spaces like motorcycling, where discernment becomes essential.

Motorcycling's history as a male-dominated space is well known, with its legacy often celebrated through the contributions of men. While those contributions deserve acknowledgment, it is just as important to recognize how male dominance has left behind patterns of misogyny[1] that continue to shape the culture today.

---

1. Misogyny: hatred of, aversion to, or prejudice against women. It is a symptom of patriarchy, reflecting not only systemic power structures but also how individuals and societies have internalized and bought into those structures. Misogyny often functions as a way people seek belonging or alignment within patriarchal norms, reinforcing a social order that harms everyone.

From the frequent sidelining of women riders at events to the lack of representation in media and industry leadership, to the condescending tone often used when women enter workshops or speak about bikes, these examples are not isolated. They are symptoms of a larger system that has colonized the original spirit of motorcycling.

Practicing discernment on this path means staying aware of how we show up in motorcycle spaces and being intentional about how we engage so we don't unknowingly replicate the very systems that seek to divide us. Whether through subtle or overt behaviors that marginalize women riders and builders, or through unchecked racism, homophobia, transphobia, and other forms of exclusion, all of these are expressions of patriarchy's lingering shadow.

These aren't just "men's issues." Internalized biases, especially internalized misogyny, live in all of us and often shape how we relate to one another. For many women, the survival strategies we developed under patriarchy taught us to turn on each other to protect the little space we were allowed. This looks like creating unnecessary competition and judgment according to the patriarchal rulebook of what is deemed worthy of respect or acceptance.

True change begins when we recognize that belonging in a so-called "man's world" doesn't require us to be hyper-independent or to compete for scraps of validation in the male gaze. Instead, we reclaim our power by choosing collaboration and co-creation with other women, with men, and with anyone else committed to building something different.

Finally, we must apply discernment to something that is often overlooked and untreated: capitalism. The prioritization of profit over people has become increasingly visible within our community. In the race for financial gain and market appeal, corporations often sacrifice authenticity and genuine connection, disguising exploitation as support.

By staying true to ourselves and to one another, we resist the pull of capitalist ideals that try to define us and dictate what we should buy. In the age of influencer culture and social media, we face the challenge of navigating systems we didn't choose while remaining mindful of the brands we represent, the products we promote, and the purchases we make.

Discernment strengthens our ability to stand united, protecting motorcycle culture from corporations that feed off our passions without giving back. When we act with intention and awareness, we safeguard the rebellious heart of this culture. We prevent it from being co-opted for profit and instead uplift businesses that truly support and expand the spirit of our community.

## The Source

You are now ready to take your remedy of nuance, hope, and discernment and apply it to the wounds within the ecosystem of motorcycling, both now and as they arise in the future.

Remember, this remedy is part of the ongoing practice of attunement to the spaces you inhabit, and you can apply it wherever you see fit.

As you prepare to pack your remedy for the road, I invite you to sit with these questions:

What was it that bikers tapped into that fueled their persistence beyond keeping their passions alive?

What gave them such conviction that life holds more than their lived experience of such oppressive and disconnected systems?

Why did they risk being metaphorically burned at the stake by mainstream society to belong to something beyond patriarchy's reach?

I believe the answers live in the truth of what it means to be fully alive. Our scars are not just reminders of past pain; they pulse with a fierce, loving vitality that binds together what was, what is, and what will be.

These scars hold the memory of power stolen but also the promise of power reclaimed.

We owe our gratitude to the bikers who came before us. Their untamed determination to carve out this counterculture has sparked a fire that still burns bright today.

It's a torch we now carry, lighting the path back to the source of the power that moved freely through this world long before patriarchy.

**I call this source the Great Mother.**

We, the Biker Witches, are Her daughters.

# Rest Area #3

Welcome to your third Rest Area. Here, you'll find questions to reflect on in your journal, many of which invite you to connect the topics from the past few chapters with your own experiences in the motorcycling community.

If you're new to motorcycling, not yet a rider, or still building your knowledge, you can respond from your perspective right now or return to the questions later when the time feels right.

**Tools You'll Need**

- A journal
- A writing utensil

1. HOW DO THE WOUNDS OF PATRIARCHY SHOW UP IN YOUR OWN EXPERIENCE OF MOTORCYCLE CULTURE OR COMMUNITY, AND WHAT FEELINGS DO THEY BRING UP?

2. IN WHAT WAYS CAN EMBRACING NUANCE CHANGE HOW YOU SEE YOURSELF AND OTHERS WITHIN THIS CULTURE?

3. WHO ARE THE TRAILBLAZERS THAT INSPIRE YOUR HOPE AND RESILIENCE? HOW CAN THEIR STORIES FUEL YOUR OWN JOURNEY?

4. WHERE DO YOU NOTICE PATTERNS OF EXCLUSION, FEAR, OR DIVISION IN YOUR COMMUNITY, AND HOW MIGHT DISCERNMENT HELP YOU RESPOND DIFFERENTLY?

5. WHAT SMALL ACTS OF HEALING, CONNECTION, OR RESISTANCE CAN YOU COMMIT TO AS YOU CARRY THIS REMEDY FORWARD ON THE ROAD?

6. WHAT ASPECTS OF MOTORCYCLE CULTURE HAVE FELT LIKE MEDICINE FOR YOU AND WHAT PARTS HAVE FELT LIKE WOUNDING? HOW DO YOU DISCERN THE DIFFERENCE?

7. WHEN HAVE YOU FELT MOST FREE ON THE ROAD? WHAT CONDITIONS, INTERNAL OR EXTERNAL, MADE THAT FREEDOM POSSIBLE?

8. HOW HAVE YOU PARTICIPATED, KNOWINGLY OR UNKNOWINGLY, IN GATEKEEPING OR UPHOLDING HARMFUL NORMS WITHIN YOUR COMMUNITY? WHAT MIGHT ACCOUNTABILITY AND REPAIR LOOK LIKE?

9. WHAT DOES IT MEAN TO YOU TO RECLAIM POWER IN A WORLD THAT OFTEN DEFINES POWER THROUGH DOMINATION OR CONTROL?

10. IF YOU WERE TO DECOLONIZE THE MOTORCYCLING COMMUNITY AND RECLAIM ITS ORIGIN STORY THROUGH A LENS OF HEALING, INCLUSION, AND REBELLION, WHAT THEMES OR TRUTHS WOULD YOU CARRY INTO YOUR OWN PARTICIPATION IN THE CULTURE?

# MOTHERLINE MAGIC

No matter where you are on your spiritual journey, whether you consider yourself an experienced practitioner of some kind or are simply exploring new spiritual terrain, the concept of a *source* of power can feel elusive, maybe even abstract.

Rest assured, you already know Her.

Picture yourself at a massive motorcycle meetup. The parking lot is packed with bikes of every make and model, and the air buzzes with the sound of engines and conversation. You're walking around, meeting fellow riders, exchanging nods, chatting about gear, swapping road stories. The interactions are lovely, just nothing out of the ordinary

Then you meet that one rider.

They notice the subtle details on your bike and ask about the story behind your favorite patch. They tell you about the winding backroad they discovered last week and how it felt like riding through a dream. You share a laugh about an inside joke that seems impossible to have with someone you've just met.

For a moment, they make you feel completely seen, as if you've been riding together for years. Then, just as suddenly, they're gone. They hop on their bike, kick up the stand, and ride off without a word, leaving you with nothing but the sound of their engine fading in the distance and the memory of a connection that felt like magic.

That's what it's like to encounter the Great Mother.

The Great Mother is Nature incarnate. She is both the earth and the primordial breath that flows within it. She is both the promise held in the seed and the rich nutrients in the dirt. She is both the marrow deep within the bone and the flesh that gives it form.

Her blood is the vital force[1] woven through all that is. It courses through the veins of the world as the living intelligence[2] within every leaf, every body, and every gust of wind.

Many modern spiritual teachings speak in terms of masculinity and femininity, framing Nature as a duality, but She is not the balance of opposites. She is the totality.

Every flower, every breeze, and every animal that crosses our path carries Her spark. She is the connective tissue that animates the entire web of life, the substance and the motion, the Matriarch, and the body[3] from which we are born and to which we all eventually return.

Her daughters, the Biker Witches, especially know Her well. She's the pulse we feel within the mountain ranges we ride through on two wheels, and the storm that warns us to pull over and let Her pass.

She's the tides and currents along the coastline we ride beside, mirroring the rhythms of our own bodies.

She lives within the steady hands of our grandmothers, whose own stories of adventure inspire us to live a life on the road, and in the seasonal cycles of birth, death, and rebirth that guide our rituals.

**Within Her, we find both our origins and our belonging.**

---

1. Power, as previously defined in *Find Your Footing*. The Great Mother is the source and origin of this power, which naturally flows through all of us.

2. Living intelligence: the conscious, responsive, and creative *expression* of power that guides the ways life sustains itself.

3. While patriarchy is the "manufactured reality" we navigate today, the Great Mother is the primordial "body of reality" that exists beyond harmful systems.

If you travel far enough through time, you'll find countless civilizations have honored Her through song, story, statue, sacrifice, and more.

We never fully see Her, yet we sense Her in the archetypes of Goddesses and Witches passed down through generations.

We never fully hear Her, yet we listen for Her in cautionary tales warning us not to stray too far into the dark woods.

We never fully touch Her, yet we feel Her when our intuition tells us to slow down just before a sharp curve.

Patriarchy has long sought to distance us from Her, but we've always found ways to keep Her close. Sometimes we meet Her in our most difficult moments—in the raw sensations of loss, childbirth, or grief—when we're unsure if we'll ever rise from the depths of our pain.

She shows up in the incandescent rage that erupts at the sight of systemic injustice and in the fire that moves us to tear it all down and build something better.

She reveals Herself in flashes of bliss and wonder, in the orgasmic rush of life's pleasures, in the fierce love of a mother, or the tender comfort we felt as children being held by our own.

These moments of contact are what patriarchal systems fear most, because when we feel ourselves held by Her, we remember that life was never meant to be avoided, abused, or subdued, but fully lived, trusted, and felt in all its fire and tenderness.

We are making our way back to a remembered life, and it's the spirits we work with who guide and support us along that path. Every spirit is a sovereign being with their own will, personality, and unique gifts, yet all of these arise from Her vital force, just as ours does.

This truth doesn't diminish our individuality within the web of life; it deepens it. The living intelligence we each carry and the power we exchange are expressions of Her presence within us.

Through our relationships with the spirits, we participate in the sacred, reciprocal flow of Her power, which moves through countless forms, shaped by our own consciousness, and expressed in infinite ways.

We offer the spirits our vulnerability, our stories, and our nourishment. In return, they offer insight, abilities, healing, guidance, and answers from deep within the more mysterious workings of nature and our lives as part of it.

This mutual sharing sustains ecological and spiritual balance by keeping power circulating through acts of reciprocity. It also reminds us that there is no hierarchy in nature; every being has something special to offer the next, and that is a profoundly beautiful truth.

Spirits nurture and expand the living intelligence already alive within you by offering what is alive within them. Through these relationships, you become shaped into a witch who lives fully within Her pulse, embodying both the reality She is and the life your ancestors once lived long ago.

## The Motherline

Before we can embrace the life that awaits us, we must pause. Just as we attuned ourselves to the ecosystem of motorcycling by noticing what needed healing, we must now turn that same attention inward, toward our own roots.

Unnamed wounds carried silently through our lineages can hinder us from fully showing up in our relationships with spirits. By understanding our ancestral inheritance and tending to these hidden wounds, we can prevent them from shaping our path and meet spirits with greater agency, clarity, and integrity.

While all of our ancestors bear the scars of patriarchy, our foremothers carry a unique and heavier burden. Patriarchy wasn't only built on their wounds; it depends on the ongoing enforcement of those wounds to persist.

To fully embody the reality of the Great Mother, we must first turn our attention to the **motherline:** the long line of women who birthed us, shaped us, and passed down Her wisdom, Her magic, and Her memory through flesh and blood.

Our bodies come from their bodies, stretching back thousands of years to the very first maternal ancestor who emerged directly from Her.

The motherline is both the biological and spiritual cord that connects us to Her. It's the heart of our ancestral magic—the essential organ that keeps the whole system alive. This cord is where mystery meets matter, and where possibility becomes tangible.

Extending from this heart are the veins of our other spiritual connections: our spirit relationships, emotional bonds, ancestral lines beyond the motherline, and the intentional practices that grow from them.

When the motherline beats strong, the lifeblood of the Great Mother flows freely through us all. When it is wounded, blocked, or ignored, no amount of surface healing can fully restore our direct link to Her. We can't simply patch collapsed channels of connection without first restoring the heart.

To begin this restoration, we must first name the wounds patriarchy has inflicted on our motherline. Then, because this system is both cultural and physiological—permeating our bodies as much as our histories—we must commit to a regular, somatic[4] practice that heals these wounds and keeps the motherline strong, shielding it from patriarchy's ongoing influence. What I've created here as a witchcraft practice for Biker Witches is designed to center this work.

The motherline was the doorway to my own spiritual path. It began with the women who came before me. Their stories, their

---

4. Somatic: Relating to the body, especially as distinct from the mind; in this context, a practice that engages the body's felt experience to process, heal, and integrate trauma or inherited patterns.

heartbreaks, and their strength became the path I followed home to Her. In the spirit of naming and tending, I invite you to sit beside me now as I share my own motherline story.

.+

I was 23 when I found myself sitting on that bathroom floor, but that moment was the final eruption after ten years of running my nervous system on autopilot. Leading up to it, there were times when the autopilot would malfunction, and the reality of my unhappiness would hit me.

I knew I needed to make hard choices, but every time I tried to summon the courage to speak my truth, fear took over. My body trembled, sometimes to the point of vomiting. I felt unrecognizable to myself, disconnected from my spirit in ways I hadn't imagined possible.

I was unwell, and I knew it. After studying human development in college, I understood the impact of childhood trauma on a person's life. What I couldn't grasp was how that same trauma was still running the show for me years later.

I knew psychology in theory, but I couldn't see how my own experiences had taught me to believe that making choices for myself—especially ones that might disappoint or hurt others—would cause everything around me to collapse, leaving no survivors.

I felt frozen and stuck. Thankfully, not long after my moment of eruption, I met a witch named Sadee Whip. She made me tea and sat with me as I poured out the grief of my childhood and the sense of powerlessness it had left me with as an adult.

She encouraged me to take a loving, but realistic look at why my nervous system had been wired to believe that others' survival depended on my ability to carry their weight, even if it meant I could never truly breathe again.

Why my mind convinced me that if I dared to climb out of rock bottom to seek the air I so desperately needed, people would die. Why, in my body, it felt safer to live a life without choices than to make decisions that might bring dire consequences.

She then suggested I begin finding my answers by exploring the very first relationship I ever knew: my relationship with my mother. For most women, this bond, whether strong or strained, shapes a foundational part of who we are.

It influences our attachment styles, our worldview, how we care for others, and how we move through the world. While some women share nurturing, loving connections with their mothers, others do not. Either way, this relationship often holds valuable insights into ourselves.

During this time in my life, I was not only facing personal struggles but also navigating the intense growing pains of early womanhood. As I reflected on who my mother was and the nature of our relationship while she was alive, that reflection began to overlap with my own personal challenges.

I felt increasingly worn down by the weight of societal expectations pressing on every part of my life—my identity, my body, my relationships, and my future. It seemed as though nothing was left untouched.

Together, these experiences helped me see my mother in a new light, not just as "Mom," but as a whole, complex person with her own hardships, dreams, and an innocence beneath the layers of armor she wore just to get through her days.

## Lorrie Lynn

Lorrie Lynn was a 5'1" storm that boomed with fury and flame, with long red hair and flair to match. She was the kind of presence you savored from a covered front porch with a fresh cup of coffee in hand. Her laughter lit up the sky like lightning, and her temper rumbled through the air like thunder.

Every time she moved, she filled you with awe and a deep appreciation for each fleeting moment; being near her was like standing inside a charge of crackling static electricity.

Her love for life was limitless, and her love for her children stretched even further. She took immense pride in raising the three of us, showing it every day through countless acts of love and unwavering ferocity.

As her youngest child and only daughter, I was always by her side, accompanying her wherever she went. I watched her closely, knowing deep down that all I ever wanted was to be just like her.

Because I was always with her, I witnessed the full spectrum of her humanity. I saw her moments of childlike wonder and joy in simple pleasures alongside her stubbornness and occasional selfishness. She lived life on her own terms, even when it meant disrupting or inconveniencing others.

She was far from perfect. She made mistakes and sometimes caused great hurt through her actions. In many ways, my mother embodied the multifaceted nature of the Great Mother, revealing Herself through forces that nurture and heal but also hold the power to harm.

She didn't have the tools to navigate this complexity, and because of that, she often struggled with extremes. Her moods would shift unexpectedly, and although she was usually gentle and peaceful, there were times when she became a tornado of unpredictability.

Unresolved childhood trauma shaped her choices in adulthood, especially in her romantic relationships. After my parents' divorce, she became involved in a highly toxic relationship with a man who amplified these mood swings, and they both relied on substance abuse to diffuse the tension.

Their toxic dynamic eventually reached a breaking point, and she sought support for her substance use after one of their separations. I remember this as the first moment I realized how patriarchal systems fail to support vulnerable people in our society.

When she was released from the rehabilitation center, there were no established protocols to help her reintegrate into her former life with new habits like sobriety. She was discharged directly back into the arms that had first led her to rehab. Her relapse happened soon after his return, with old patterns quickly resurfacing between them.

Eventually, the toxicity between them became unbearable, and he left her, leaving her heartbroken. She continued drinking and leaning on anything that would temporarily ease her sorrow. To make matters worse, those who should have shown her a love that holds toughness—an accountability for everyone involved, which an addicted person sometimes needs—instead enabled and participated in her habits.

My mother's spiral quickly picked up pace. She was disoriented, trying to find her way in a society that slaps band-aids over deep wounds without ever addressing the source of the bleeding. She was lost and grieving, and I have no doubt she felt the walls closing in around her.

Familiar faces began to turn away to protect their own peace, reflecting the colonial impulse to abandon those who struggle in the name of self-preservation and the illusion of normalcy. She fought to survive, but the weight of it all grew too heavy to carry alone.

In the heat of a moment triggered by yet another betrayal, she made the fatal decision to get behind the wheel after a long night of drinking, and it cost her *everything*.

I share the tragic ending of my mother's life not because I think it's important for you to know how she died, but to help you understand why she is no longer here—why she isn't physically present in her children's lives or in the lives of the granddaughters she never got to meet.

This story isn't meant to cast my mother as a victim or those around her as villains. Life is far more complicated than that. She had some truly amazing friends who tried to help.[5]

They offered support, shared resources, listened, and even stepped in to care for us when she couldn't. For that, I will always be deeply grateful. But it still wasn't enough, and that's not their fault either.

The devastating rage I feel over her death comes from knowing that if patriarchy had never taken hold, things could have been different. Everyone would have access to the power and roles needed to sustain the collective ecosystem of care that once thrived before colonization.

Communities would be well-resourced, so the responsibility of supporting someone in crisis could be shared among many instead of resting on just a few shoulders.

In that world, healing wouldn't be reduced to temporary fixes inside a system designed to knock people back down the moment they begin to rise. Gifted souls like hers wouldn't be sacrificed to patriarchal standards that prioritize hyper-individualism over genuine connection and care.

My mother would still be alive, enjoying her life past the age of 42, deepening into her magic instead of being consumed by her wounds.

After reflecting on who my mother was and how her story unfolded, I took an honest look at our relationship. She was my best friend, but at times our bond blurred into enmeshment. From a very young age, I felt responsible for her well-being in ways no child should.

I thought back to the night she died—the same night I had gone to my father's house for the weekend. At that moment, I found the answer to Sadee's questions:

---

5. Thank you Michele Bennett and Dorothy Rusby. I will never forget everything you did for my family. I love you both.

**The belief that leaving any situation, even one that was toxic or beyond repair, was simply not an option. If I chose myself and stepped away to live my own life, people would die.**

That was the story my body believed. It was written into my nervous system, convincing me that staying put in a life I hated was the only way to keep others safe.

## Following the Motherline

I wanted to understand more, so I set that epiphany aside for a moment and turned my attention to my grandmother. If my struggles came from losing my mother, then my mother's likely came from losing hers.

I already knew my mother had died carrying what looked like unhealed wounds, but I began to wonder if my grandmother's death held a similar story.

My Nana, Hilda, was my mother's favorite person in the world. I was young when she died, but I remember it clearly. She passed away six years before my mother, at just 56, after a battle with ovarian cancer.

Her womb, the same one that brought my mother into this world, had become poisoned. This led me to think not just about her death, but about her life.[6]

Everyone who knew Nana described her as the hardest-working woman they had ever met. As a single mother, she held down multiple jobs to put food on the table and raise both my mother and my aunt. She cared for everyone around her and rarely, if ever, made space for her own needs or desires.

In a capitalist society that glorifies overworking, burnout is worn like a badge of honor. But in the process, her light dimmed and her power was drained. She gave endlessly and received little in

---

6. In many spiritual cosmologies, a woman's womb is believed to hold creative and generative power, and when unwell, can offer insight into the person's life and experiences.

return, and her life was cut tragically short before she had the chance to truly live for herself.

Moving up the motherline, I thought about Nana's mother, my great-grandmother, also named Hilda. She died just three months after Nana's passing, likely from a broken heart.

I realized that within six years, I had lost the last surviving women of my motherline. That moment marked a turning point. It was the epiphany that set me on a path to seek answers, and it was then that I first learned about the epigenetics of the maternal line.

Science now shows that a woman's lived experiences can ripple through at least three generations, weaving the past, present, and future together in significant ways. As Mark Wolynn explains in *It Didn't Start With You: How Inherited Family Trauma Shapes Who We Are and How to End the Cycle*:

> When your grandmother was five months pregnant with your mother, the precursor cell of the egg you developed from was already present in your mother's ovaries. This means that before your mother was even born, your mother, your grandmother, and the earliest traces of you were all in the same body—three generations sharing the same biological environment (25).

This understanding revealed that the wounds in my motherline were shaped not only by personal struggles, but also by experiences inherited long before any of us were born. My life was influenced not just by my mother's story, but also by my grandmother's, whose life in turn was shaped by her mother's, and so on, tracing all the way back through generations to the very origins of our maternal line.

As I examined my family's patterns more closely, a painful trend emerged: nearly every woman on my mother's side either died at 56 or younger, or, if still alive, battles chronic illness or addiction.

Those who escaped these extremes still carry the heavy weight of loss and the lingering fear that they may be next. Many have coped by choosing sobriety or making significant medical decisions, like hysterectomies or mastectomies, as preventative measures shaped by both our genetic inheritance and a long history of heartache.

I began tracing the roots of my maternal ancestors, uncovering the threads of my motherline that run through Ireland, Wales, and Scotland. These are lands with rich and complex histories, unsurprisingly marked by colonization and patriarchal control. As I dug deeper, I discovered that matrilineal traditions once thrived in these regions.

Women held central and respected roles within their communities, and the strength of the female family line was revered. Over time, patriarchy disrupted these traditions, shifting power away from women and concentrating it in the hands of men. The impact of that disruption rippled through generations, severing our access to the Great Mother and blocking the flow of ancestral magic within my motherline.

As a result, the women in my family were left repeatedly exploited, silenced, and unsupported by systems built to diminish their power. Their wholeness, vitality, and potential were gradually eroded by patriarchy. This legacy reveals itself through the epigenetic markers of chronic illness, disease expressed through addiction, and early death.

It became clear to me why claiming agency over my own life felt like a matter of life or death. The fear I felt was not mine alone. It was entangled with the fears of the women who came before me. Every time I faced the choice to lay claim to my own fate, it stirred memories of desperation to survive that were embedded in my cells.

My nervous system could not separate my trauma from theirs. I wasn't only carrying my own experiences; I was carrying the unhealed wounds of every woman in my maternal line. I had unknowingly inherited generations of warnings telling me not to rock the boat in life, because if I did, it would sink and drown everyone aboard, including me.

I believe the shock from the sudden loss of my mother opened the floodgates to those messages. I carried them into early adulthood until I was faced with the truth that ignoring them would eventually lead me to the same fate.

Looking back now, I don't see my mother as someone who failed to heal. Instead, I see a woman who carried the weight of generations, yet still managed to carve out moments of happiness, creativity, and wonder amidst it all.

I also believe she absorbed as much of our motherline trauma as she could before passing anything on to me. Her willingness to bear that burden gave me the chance to live a life she wasn't able to finish, and **her love lives on in my ability to now choose a different way forward.**

## A New Legacy

I was furious when I uncovered the countless ways the women in my family had been denied long, fulfilling, and healthy lives. The weight of generational hardship, compounded by systems designed to break them, had in fact broken them. My anger was, and is, truly raging.

But alongside that anger came relief. I began to see that the struggles I faced were not personal failings or signs of weakness. My fear of making difficult decisions was both a trauma response and a survival mechanism, carried in the cellular memories of my motherline, revealing the resilience of nature and of women alike.

We are the reflection of the Great Mother's enduring strength, and we pass that adaptability down through generations.

I carried this fury and relief back into my own life. I knew I needed to find a new way forward, but if I could no longer carry the weight of loss, what could I carry instead?

I thought of the times when my mother seemed most alive. It was always when she was riding her motorcycle or practicing her witchcraft. I believe these two things sustained her and kept her holding on to life for as long as she could. That was when she was most radiant. That was when she was fully Lorrie.

I chose to embrace those same things. First, I leaned into ritual and began an ancestor practice, making offerings, asking questions, and listening for guidance from the women who came before me. Then, I learned how to ride, and everything changed.

By combining these worlds, I found a way to reimagine my life, even in the face of fear and beneath the weight of the guilt of choosing myself. I stepped beyond pain and into something greater: a new legacy born of rebellion, joy, and sovereignty[7].

## Our Shared Motherline Story

My motherline story isn't unique. Though the close losses I endured so quickly may be rare, the memories of a life once lived in alignment with the Great Mother, and the ways that life was fractured, remain in all of us.

If every woman traced her motherline far enough, she would likely uncover remnants of matriarchal wisdom and traditions that honored women in their communities. As Pixie notes in the foreword of this book, these traditions are rare today and are often overshadowed or redirected by systemic forces to serve oppressive structures.

In place of those traditions, women have been given a new set of parameters for participating in the fate of their own lives. We are given just enough space to survive, but rarely enough to thrive or fully break free of patriarchy.

---

7. Sovereignty: the full embodiment of autonomy, self-determination, and authority over one's life, choices, and body. To be sovereign is to live in alignment with one's personal values and desires, free from the control, dictates, and limitations imposed by patriarchal systems.

We are expected to work tirelessly, hold families together, nurture those around us, and manage the emotional and physical labor of daily life, all while being denied access to decision-making roles that could shape the communities and systems that govern us.

We are encouraged to compete with one another, tearing each other down instead of building each other up, all to weaken our collective power. When we claim autonomy over our bodies and lives, we are often labeled selfish or ungrateful, sometimes even by the people we care about.

The wisdom passed down through generations of women is dismissed as irrelevant, overly emotional, or too radical. Our voices are silenced in boardrooms, in science, medicine, education, politics, and in every space where decisions that affect our lives and futures are made.

Within patriarchy, the very essence of being a woman—our strength, intuition, and capacity for transformative change—is constantly undermined. Cultural narratives make it hard to imagine or pursue lives that fully empower us. Instead, we remain trapped in cycles of self-sacrifice and resignation, passing patterns of systemic wounding through the motherline for generations.

## The Ritual

We honor all of our ancestors by learning about their lives, the lands they came from, and the ways they shaped the world, but it is only when the motherline's magic flows freely again that we can fully step into our relationships as witches and steer the fate of our own lives as women.

This is where our Biker Witch practice truly takes shape.

The first step in restoring the flow is remembering. We piece together the story of our motherline by naming what was, what could have been, and what still might be. We gather the fragments, the silences, and the inherited grief, weaving them into a broader understanding that helps us discern what trauma comes from our own experiences living within patriarchy, and what has been passed down from the women before us.

As we look at these pieces, we ask ourselves: How do we carry our foremothers' histories without letting them define us? How do we hold the truth of the past without letting it take control of the ride?

This is when we begin to live the repair.

We take these stories with us on the road. We ride with them in our bodies, in our breath, in the hum of the engine. We let them move through us and speak truths we couldn't hear while standing still.

The road teaches us to hold their stories with reverence, not as burdens; to witness their suffering without reenacting it; to integrate the lessons and resilience while letting their pain exhale through us and be carried away by the wind.

The balance between holding on and letting go becomes the steady cadence of our practice. For us as Biker Witches, that cadence lives in motion.

The ride itself becomes ritual.

Every ride guides us to return to what was lost, what still aches, and what longs to be remembered. We carry our own wounds, questions, and dreams alongside those of our foremothers.

With every twist of the throttle, we open ourselves as channels, letting the Great Mother move through us to loosen what has been stuck for generations. We give ourselves permission to shed layers of inherited ache and feel Her instead.

We ride with our foremothers as our passengers—a collective voice in our ear reminding us that we're allowed to go further than they ever could.

Returning, honoring, and releasing creates a cycle that frees the weight of the past and consistently nourishes the motherline, shielding it from patriarchy.

This is the heart of our witchcraft practice.

Consistent ritual born from the ride, sustained by the desire to honor the women who came before us and reclaim all that was taken from them.

This ritual transforms us, not only spiritually but biologically. Practices rooted in reverence and hope help the brain form new, healing associations about our lineage. As these neural pathways develop, they influence stress responses and emotional patterns.

Over time, these shifts can affect the epigenetic tags that regulate how our genes respond to stress, providing a biological pathway through which ritual can influence inherited patterns (Wolynn, 52). In this way, ritual can help interrupt trauma passed down through the motherline, dismantling cycles that have carried through generations.

In other words, we quite literally become the ones who change the story.

We become cycle breakers on the road.

We release the pain our foremothers were forced to carry, clearing the way for Her lifeblood to move freely once more.

We become Biker Witches, wholly living our **motherline magic.**

# Rest Area #4

Welcome to your fourth Rest Area. Here, you'll begin to piece together the story of your motherline. This story helps you name both the pain and the power in your maternal lineage. It also reveals the patterns that shape your life and helps you discern what is truly yours and what has been passed down.

For some, the biological motherline may be unknown or unclear through adoption or other paths, and that is fully honored here. This work also holds space for the women who have shaped and supported us beyond bloodlines, recognizing that the circle of feminine wisdom and care often extends wider than biology alone.

If at any point you feel this exercise is too painful, pause and return when you feel safe to revisit. It may even be helpful to review our pre-ride safety checklist before beginning this exercise.

Next, you'll be guided through a meditative ritual that calls your foremothers into your life, inviting them to ride with you as you transform the inherited pain into power and strengthen the flow of the motherline.

They will become your passengers, ready to cheer you on and offer protection. Wrapped in a blanket of love woven through generations of resilience, you will ride with them, held, witnessed, and never alone.

## Tools You'll Need

- A journal

- A writing utensil

- A candle, incense, or anything that helps you root into a meditative space

- Something comfortable to sit on

- Optional: photos, letters, or heirlooms from your motherline ancestors

## Setting the Container

- Prepare your space with intention

- Light a candle or incense to mark your entry into sacred time

- Take a few grounding breaths

- Feel the earth beneath you, holding you steady

- Let yourself arrive, fully and just as you are

# Piecing Together Your Motherline Story

## 1. Begin With What You Know

In your journal, write down the names of the women in your maternal line beginning with the name of the woman who carried you, then her mother, and those before her.

If you don't know their names, write what you do know. Include stories, memories, or impressions. If you don't know anything, that's absolutely okay. Even silence holds meaning here.

## 2. Name The Pain and The Power

Reflect on the grief, challenges, or patterns that may have moved through this line. This can include personal wounds passed from mother to daughter, conflicts within families, or the broader systemic harms that have scarred your ancestors.

When you're ready, shift into the power. What resilience or magic lives in this line? In what ways do you carry these gifts?

## 3. Discern What is Yours

Notice which parts of this story feel like they belong to you. What might you still be carrying that is no longer yours to hold? What wisdom do you want to claim and carry forward?

## 4. Spend time with what connects you

If you have photos, letters, or heirlooms, take a few quiet minutes with them. Notice the faces of the women in the images, the way their handwriting curves and flows across the page, and how these objects that carry years of memories feel in your hands.

## 5. Invite them in

**Note:** If your foremothers don't feel safe to you yet, it's completely okay to wait on this invitation. Take the time you need to move through this work and build your own process with them. You are in control of this journey. Invite them when you're ready.

Close your eyes and take a deep breath. Imagine yourself sitting on your bike on a long, open road stretching endlessly before you. The air is soft, warm, and gentle. Around you, the landscape is vast and still.

Far off, you sense movement. Slowly, one by one, your foremothers begin to appear. Some faces feel familiar, perhaps from more recent lifetimes. Others are mysterious and unknown, from eras hundreds or even thousands of years past.

With steady steps, they approach you without words, yet their silence speaks volumes. One by one, they reach out with warm hands, one resting on your shoulder and the other gently on your heart, steadying your breath. Each touch carries a story of love fiercely given, of sorrow endured, of unyielding pride.

They look into your eyes with a quiet invitation, an unspoken plea to join you on this journey. You offer your bike freely. One by one, they climb on behind you, their arms wrapping around you in a protective embrace.

Their presence becomes the wind at your back, a steady force moving you forward. They ride with you not just to release their pain, but to protect you. They hold you in ways that remind you that you are never truly alone.

Let this image settle deep into your body. Breathe with them. Feel their hearts beating in rhythm with yours. Their love, their strength, and their courage woven into your very being, carrying you onward through the road ahead.

## 6. Close with gratitude

Take a final deep breath, and whisper your thanks to the women who showed up.

Gently return to the space around you, and write down anything that came through during the meditation in your journal.

# A Biker Witch is Born

Bikers everywhere move through the world engaging with mysterious forces, often without even realizing it. Spirit bells hang from our bikes, warding off mischievous beings. Words like *Harley-Davidson* become incantations that summon adventure, while patches stitched to our leathers signal to the ecosystem who we are and where we've been.

Our riding rituals, protective charms, and shared superstitions reflect the understanding that there is more to this world than what meets the eye. Motorcycle culture is steeped in magic, yet not everyone rides the path of the Biker Witch. This route isn't for everyone, and that's okay. For those of us who do, it's because She pulled us here.

## The Call

The Great Mother calls us home in a language beyond words. For most of us, this call begins long before we ever hear it. The spirits have always been part of our lives, tending our path and offering gentle nudges that open the door to a life beyond the confines of patriarchy.

But like being born into a cage, most of us have only ever known the walls that surround us. Even when we long to fly freely, we learn to bend ourselves into the shape of constraint. We become experts at numbing our intuition, finding ways to compartmentalize the truth that life was never meant to be this way.

It isn't until something completely shatters our reality that we finally hear Her. A point of crisis—an illness, a loss, a burnout, a deep grief—brings our world to a screeching halt, leaving us suddenly face-to-face with what we've ignored for years.

When we realize there is nowhere else to go, no mask left to wear, no other numbing solution, we are left with no choice but to really feel our lives.

What follows is less a decision than an exhausted surrender. We collapse into the arms of the Great Mother, and She pulls us into Her embrace.

Here begins our initiation.

The birth of the Biker Witch within.

## The Pull

When the Great Mother finally pulls us closer to Her, it can feel like we're free-falling through open space. It's disorienting, even jarring, because it's the first time we're letting life move fully *through* us.

Her primordial current tosses and turns us, doing whatever is necessary to pull us back into alignment with the web of life. On the surface, it might seem like we're flailing, but what feels like chaos is actually the Great Mother moving us toward exactly what we need to become an active participant in this process.

As She pulls, we are also compelled to confront what we have long avoided, and that can feel overwhelming. We are forced to experience our lives fully, to meet grief, loss, and endings we may have spent years avoiding. It could be saying goodbye to a relationship, mourning the death of a loved one, or releasing a past self we can no longer carry into who we're becoming.

Fear, attachment, and buried sorrow rise to the surface, demanding to be seen and honored. The sensation is raw and unyielding, yet it is in this surrender to feeling that we find the depth, courage, and resilience to move freely with life.

Like a loving mother, the Great Mother draws us toward what can support us through this moment of reckoning. Think of a time when a personal crisis forced you to surrender, to trust that life would carry you forward, and then, almost without warning, led you to something new: a hobby, a subject, a place, a person.

It probably seemed random at the time, but later you realized it was precisely what you needed most. Perhaps it opened a new sense of wonder for the world around you, or gave you the courage to make changes you had long been avoiding.

The moment we surrender to Her initiatory pull is paradoxical. It asks us to release control without losing agency. It requires us to let life unravel while still holding an essential role in what happens within the unraveling.

That metaphysical space between surrender and sovereignty is both challenging and exhilarating, laying the groundwork we need as witches who work closely with spirits. Lucy H. Pearce captures this paradox with piercing clarity in *Burning Woman*:

> Within the course of our lives we pass through a thousand deaths, losses big and small—of identities and loved ones, places and people. Our death and rebirth to the Feminine is one of the biggest. Through this experience we learn the truth that death never is The End, but always leads to rebirth, and new existence in a different form. We discover that what we had feared as final annihilation is actually an integral part of the creative process. This helps us to release our fear and resistance, and begin to lean into the divine paradox, embracing the reality that in death lies life, in creativity lies destruction. When we do, what emerges is the

freedom to fully and creatively engage with the miracle that is life, bringing the full power which lies within us into the world, during our brief journey from the womb of our mother to the womb of the Earth (93).

For Biker Witches, embracing our own cycles of death and rebirth lies at the heart of our homecoming. Often, a crisis wakes us, followed by surrender that allows parts of ourselves to fall away and create space for something new.

Pearce reminds us:

> Often we long for "spiritual" experiences to "raise our consciousness" or "empower" us, but when they come, they are very different to what we expect. We have been led to expect that spiritual experiences are when we are touched by the light and transformed. When actually far more spiritual experience takes place in the dark. A cursory flick through the stories of spiritual transformation in any of the major sacred texts will quickly show you that the road to spiritual power is littered with trials, exile, infertility, loss, disability, wrestling angels and wandering in the desert. Each breaking open, each initiation into the underworld through grief, illness, depression, anxiety or loss—is a potential initiation, a portal of possibility where we get the chance to see and feel the very root of our own fire in the deepest dark (101-02).

The path of the Biker Witch is the fire found in the darkness, the magic reclaimed from the wreckage of our initiations. On the road and in the deep night of the soul, we are reborn.

## The Transformation

Within the liminal space between who we once were and who we're becoming, we are tender and vulnerable, held by the Great Mother. In this embrace, She cracks open the hardened shell we built to survive patriarchy, revealing the wings we always had but had long forgotten how to use.

We are freed from the cage, reconnected with our cyclical nature, and realigned with the eternal forces of creation, destruction, and renewal—gaining a bird's-eye view of the world.

From this vantage, we see how deliberately patriarchy has stripped mystery from our lives, insisting that only what is visible, measurable, and rational is valid, while dismissing dreams, discrediting instinct, and denying the spirits who have always walked beside us.

Sadee Whip, author of *Savage Awakening: Initiatory Paths of the Dragon Mother*, calls this phenomenon the Field of Denial:

> For modern westerners, it shows up as denying that we are in the circle of life, that we are not the center. It means denying we are integrated with life, instead of in control of it. It means denying that scary or bad things happen, no matter how hard we pray, how many affirmations we say, who we pray to. It means denying there are things we cannot know. It means denying that there are strange and unknowable powers in this world that cannot be understood, measured, studied, or controlled through science or rationalism. It means denying that we are a multiplicity, formed and informed, by all that we encounter, utterly dependent on the web in which we belong (93).

It is this denial that upholds the systems keeping us isolated and disconnected from Her. Initiation gives us the push we need to finally break free from them, to let go of the illusion of control, and to surrender to the unknown.

When we do, our entire sense of place in the world shifts. We are no longer separate or superior. We remember we are part of the circle of life, and we are brought back to where our ancestors once knew they belonged.

## The Vehicle

All of us likely have a moment we can pinpoint when we first heard the call, when surrender rose up inside us, when we were pulled somewhere else, and when the transformation became undeniable. Each person carries a unique story around their initiation.

For Biker Witches, one truth remains constant: motorcycles are always a crucial part of this story.

The motorcycle can appear in our lives at any point along this call-pull-transformation process. For non-riders, the call might appear as a spark of curiosity when they hear an engine rumble across a parking lot, or as the sudden confidence to ride on the back of a friend's bike. It might take the form of attending a riding class on a whim, only to realize they're literally steering their life with their own hands—an autonomy they've never felt before.

The call can also come to someone who is already riding. They may have known the power of the open road for years, yet something inside them begins to feel the tension between how they feel on the bike and how they're expected to live within patriarchy. That unbearable contradiction becomes an inner signal that something needs to shift, ultimately leading to a pull toward something deeper.

For others, motorcycles are part of the pull. A woman in crisis might see another woman ride past at a stoplight and recognize herself in that rider, sparking a curiosity that leads her to sign up for a class. She might be navigating a broken heart and feel something lift inside her the first time she smells fuel in the morning air, feeling the strange certainty that motorcycles are part of her destiny.

For me, the path unfolded after a surrender and a pull, as part of my own transformation. A major rupture forced me to confront my life in a way I had never dared before. In that surrender, I felt broken, but I was also pulled toward what I truly needed: ancestral reclamation.

Ancestral reclamation changed the way I moved through the world. It made me more curious and inspired me to dig deeper. In exploring my motherline, I discovered how much motorcycles had empowered my mother, even through her struggles.

Learning to ride became a natural extension of the work I was already doing. The motorcycle became the teacher I didn't know I needed. Every mile carried me farther from my old life and closer to Her, leading me to emerge as a Biker Witch.

This path looks different for each of us, yet the vehicle we ride it with remains the same. This reality has carried across generations. Since the earliest days of motorcycling, women have turned to the road as a form of rebirth.

The term *Biker Witch* may be new, but the spirit behind it is ancient. Long before we named it, we were already living it. We felt it every time we accelerated into the wind, every time we placed a wrench on steel, and every time an engine roared and something deep inside us answered. These were the first spells of freedom She used to call us home.

From deserts to mountains, from city streets to forest roads, Biker Witches release old stories to make space for something more true. Whether or not they call it witchcraft, they live its wisdom in every mile.

If you've found your way here, you may have already passed through your own initiation, or you may be standing at the threshold, sensing that something deeper is stirring. Either way, I hope you feel seen in this moment. Initiation can challenge us beyond measure, and it rarely feels whimsical while we're in it.

My hope is that these words can help you understand where you are in this process and remind you that you're never alone. The next chapter, *Fireside Stories*, collects moments of initiation from Biker Witches around the world.

These are their personal tales of crossing thresholds on two wheels, taking up space, finding their own fire in the darkness, rediscovering who they are outside of roles and scripts within patriarchy, breaking free from what once confined them, living their lives in ways that honor their foremothers, and weaving magic into their communities.

These women have ridden through their own initiatory fires and now offer their hands, ready to hold yours.

Come. Sit with us by the fire. The circle is open.

# FIRESIDE STORIES

 **Krista, Canada:** I believe the best way to share my journey into motorcycles is to begin with what my life was like before I found them, because that contrast is a defining part of my story. On the surface, I seemed successful. I was a mortgage broker with three kids, and to the outside world, it looked like I had it all together.

But the truth was, I was deeply unhappy and lost. My addiction to drugs and alcohol touched every aspect of my life, leaving me in a dark, shame-filled place. I didn't feel good about who I was, and I was disconnected from what was missing in my life or the traumas that had brought me there. Deciding to get clean was the first step in a steep learning curve, and it changed everything. Motorcycles became the second cornerstone of my transformation.

In sobriety, I started discovering who I was—what I liked, what I didn't, what I needed more of, and what I needed to let go of. When I was using, I was so numb that none of it really mattered; the only thing that did was getting high. As I came back to myself, I made a bold decision to sell my mortgage brokerage business and walk away from a six-figure salary.

My husband's unwavering support gave me the courage to take that leap. He said, "If this is what your intuition is telling you, if this is where life is leading you and it's going to make you happy, then I'm behind you one hundred percent. Go for it."

So, I quit my job. Then, for the next six months, I did nothing but learn to ride a motorcycle. At 33, with no prior experience, I wasn't sure I could even do it. Each day, after dropping my kids off at school and seeing my husband off to work, I spent hours riding solo.

Motorcycling quickly became central to who I was. Learning to ride was challenging, but mastering something new—especially while sober—was incredibly rewarding. For the first time in years, I felt genuinely proud of myself.

I'll never forget struggling with the slalom during a weekend course, calling my husband in tears, convinced I couldn't do it. He reassured me, "You've got this. It'll click!" When it finally did, the pride I felt was overwhelming. It was the first spark of joy in my sobriety.

Motorcycles gave me a reason to feel proud, and that desire for pride started to spill into other areas of my life. It led me to create Della Crew, a unique clothing and lifestyle brand inspired by Miss Della Crewe, who, in 1914, bought a Harley Davidson on a whim and embarked on a cross-country journey with her dog, Trouble.

As I became more immersed in the motorcycle community, I realized it wasn't just about the bikes. It was about building the friendships and connections I had been missing. Della Crew grew into more than a brand; it became a celebration of the people who made it special.

The joy and pride I found through Della Crew snowballed. It inspired me to share this journey with others, especially women who might be struggling. Whether they're facing addiction or searching for a passion to ignite their lives, I wanted to help them find their spark.

Being vulnerable and open about my journey felt scary at first, but sharing my story was met with kindness and care from the motorcycle community. That acceptance encouraged me to keep going—to push myself further, to ride better, and eventually, to learn to stunt ride.

I'll admit, I'm an adrenaline seeker. Maybe motorcycles replaced the chaos of my old lifestyle, but in a way that feels healthy and fulfilling. I used to think sobriety would be boring, but that turned out to be the furthest thing from the truth.

In a male-dominated world like motorcycling, the bond between women is incredibly powerful. When you meet another woman on a bike, there's this instant connection. Like you just know, *you're my people*. Stunting deepens that bond even further. For the few women who stunt Harleys, maybe 20 of us worldwide, it feels like finding a soul sister.

Last year, we created a film for International Female Ride Day called *Looking for Trouble* to showcase the incredible female talent in our stunting community. My goal was to give these women a platform and hopefully attract sponsors to support them with parts and bikes since the men were getting that support and the women weren't. I thought, "Why aren't companies seeing you? Let's get you seen."

After the movie came out, we became even closer, and suddenly people started reaching out to book us for shows. They were talking about "our team," but we were just friends who rode together. When I shared these opportunities with the girls, they said, "Let's do it! Make the team, manage us, book it!" So, I took it on.

Though I was still new to stunting, my background in business and marketing was exactly what our team needed. I knew how to approach companies, ask for support, and negotiate partnerships. Together, our team became the complete package, on and off the bike.

I've stopped trying to control every aspect of life. Call it God, the universe, or something else, but I've learned to trust the process. I've seen enough in my life to know that when I let go and simply do the next right thing, everything falls into place naturally. Nothing is forced.

I can't orchestrate the universe and accepting that is incredibly freeing. While I don't know much about witchcraft itself, I do know there's spiritual power in everything, from small moments to massive events. This truth keeps revealing itself to me, so I've stopped fighting it. I accept that what will be, will be.

Without motorcycles and the incredible support of this community, I wouldn't be who I am today. It's not just about the rides or the achievements. It's about the feelings they bring, the way they've enriched my life.

Now, I strive to give back. I aim to be a welcoming face for other women, showing them the same kindness I was shown. Whether it's inviting someone for a ride or reminding them it's not about speed but connection, I try to pass on the lessons I've learned.

Motorcycling saved me, and the women in this community helped me rebuild my life. I owe so much to them and to this passion that has become my purpose.

⁺₊

**Serena, UK:** For years I wasn't interested in motorcycles and so resisted them because they were *his* world. My partner and I have been together for 27 years, and I've always believed it's important to maintain separate worlds—separate hobbies, friends, identities—as well as have shared interests and joys. Watching him with motorcycles was watching him be fully free, and I didn't want to encroach or change that space where he thrived.

We had children young; he was 20 and I was 19, and I fully immersed myself in being a mom. I was a full-time stay-at-home mother, baking, telling stories, gardening, and making their toys. In hindsight, I see that I gave myself over completely to feminine energy, and I loved nearly every moment.

It wasn't until a few years ago, when my partner and I took our first child-free trip to Rome, that something shifted. I'd always known I was genuinely *me*, but I'd always been the me who was "mom" first. However, that geographical distance showed me that not only were the kids surviving without me, but I was surviving without them.

It brought up the question: "Who am I now if I'm not so needed to be fully mom?"

One moment in particular stands out. We'd just arrived in Rome, and I was roasting in my jeans, hauling luggage through the cobbled streets in the heat, when I saw these glamorous women zipping in and out of traffic on their Vespas. Bright red lipstick, manicured nails, cute scarves—they looked so feminine and so badass at the same time.

Women of all ages, from young girls to elegant older ladies, owning those scooters. I thought "That looks like fun!" For the first time, I wondered if motorcycles could be *mine*, too, without becoming a copy of my partner. I realized I could remain myself, keep my crystals, my nails, stay kinda girly, and still ride.

When we got back home, I casually told my partner I might want to try the first step of motorcycle training, the CBT here in the UK. He lit up. Before I knew it, I had an email come through. He'd booked me in, and I thought, "Wow, this is really happening." It was beautiful how he didn't gate keep his world.

At 42, I learned to ride a motorcycle. It was the first hobby I'd ever pursued just for me. I've always loved my other hobbies, like cooking, gardening, making dolls for the kids, but the end result was always for someone else. Riding was different. Initially it was hard to give myself permission to do something without a practical purpose. It was difficult to accept that no one else would benefit.

But rediscovering that joy felt like finding the little kid I used to be. The one who rode her BMX over mountains of stored gravel for roadworks, built go-karts, and sped down hills on these things, hands in the air, laughing.

I passed my CBT on a little scooter—what we call a "chicken chaser." I was adamant I wanted a Vespa, something cute and what I thought was more me. When Christmas came, my partner surprised me with a black Mutt Fat Sabbath 125. I took one look and thought, "I don't fucking know how to do gears! This isn't what I imagined!"

I decided to go with the flow, and he taught me the basics in a parking lot. Soon we were riding together, finding a new connection without losing our individuality

I kept pushing myself. I saved up, passed the next two difficult (and expensive) tests, and bought a Royal Enfield, a bigger bike with more power to fully enjoy the roads. I doubted myself at times, especially after failing one test. The old thoughts crept in: "Maybe I'm too old. Maybe I should stick with what I know." I told myself this year was about doing things that scare me. I passed, and everything in my life shifted again.

The biking community welcomed me with open arms. The men are lovely, but the women—oh, they're something special. They scoop you up, take you under their wing, and there's no judgment (if there is, in my older age I've learnt to ignore it—it's theirs, not mine, to carry). Just connection.

It's humbling to start as a learner and embrace the vulnerability that comes with it.  People who've known me for years say, "She's having a midlife crisis" or, "Who does she think she is?" To that, I say, with two fingers up: "Screw you. I'm showing my kids that you can be whoever you want to be at any stage of life, and you don't have to abandon one version to be another."

Life is like a tree trunk that keeps growing. Each year adds a ring, but the core remains. I'm still me, just expanding. I still love cooking and gardening, and I love dirty bikes and the open road now too. I'm also learning that I can love being a mom and still deserve a life that's just mine.

.⁺✦

**Hex, Australia:** I've been connected to motorcycling for most of my life. My dad always rode and even far back in the family history, my grandfather's cousin was an early motorcycle racer. He raced in the first few Isle of Man TT races before it was even called Isle of Man. The love for motorcycles has always been embedded in my family, so the thought of getting my motorcycle license and purchasing my own bike as an adult didn't stand out as a new concept.

It wasn't until I finished high school, moved out from home, came to the city and met my partner that I even began considering obtaining my license. My partner got into riding, got his license, and became a racer in the time that we'd been together, but I never went out of my way to do it for myself because I always came up with reasons that I had more important things to do and put my money towards.

As the oldest daughter, I have always held the role of being the organizer. I kept my sister and my parents in line, not because it was something I decided to do on my own but because if I didn't do it, it was pure chaos. It was an expectation that was always on me, and I carried that responsibility into every facet of my life as an adult.

When my partner and I began to create our own life together, I realized this expectation was always going to hinder me if I didn't start setting some boundaries. I knew if I didn't actively try to stop this cycle, it was just going to continue.

I was about 26 or 27 when I was spending a lot of my time and energy trying to save up to buy a house. I was also managing a team at work, constantly answering phone calls from my family to act as the mediator, and I sort of naturally fell into the homemaker role around the house. It was a few years later, sometime around 2022, that I can still vividly recall the moment when I just... snapped.

I was trying to go for a new job, one that would require all my focus and energy. I knew I needed to pursue this job for myself, but I felt like I couldn't because I already had too many expectations and obligations at the time. At this moment, I realized that after the job and the house will come marriage, then kids, and I started to panic internally.

I started thinking about all the older ladies I'd met in my most formative years working in Aged Care, who had finally "begun their lives" in their eighties or nineties by taking up new hobbies now that the demands of being everybody's nurturer weren't so much of an obstacle.

I'd only just started freeing myself from the oldest daughter's responsibilities, and I felt like I was staring down the barrel of wife/mother responsibilities. It was a crushing feeling to see that the shining light at the end of the tunnel started morphing into a wall from my perspective, and I realized that I've never actually done anything for myself and only myself.

I thought to myself, okay, what do I want to do?

I decided to finally get a bike.

In Australia, specifically for my state, getting your license, getting the legally required gear, purchasing a motorcycle and registering it can be very expensive. It costs thousands upon thousands of dollars to do so. We also have different levels of licensing so it can take years to get to be where you want to be.

I took it one step at a time. I started looking at cruisers because in Australia you must start with a smaller cc bike. The licensing requirements correlate with the size bike you can have and eventually with more testing and licensing you can start getting into bigger bikes.

I opened the bike sales app and found this little white cruiser on the Gold Coast which is about an hour and a half from me. I saw that I could afford it. I never mentioned anything to my partner up until this point because it was all in my head in a chaotically wonderful way. It was that moment when you lose all sense of sanity for a minute and you decide "Fuck it, I'm just going to do whatever I want."

So, I said to him "What are we doing today? He said, "I think we were just gonna do some stuff in the garden." I said, "well, look, there's this Suzuki Boulevard. It's on bike sales. It's on the Gold Coast and I wouldn't mind going to check it out." He was like "Oh, okay, let's go!"

We went to check it out and I said "Yep, I love this bike." and he said, "Are you sure you don't want to look at something else?" and I said "Nope. I want this bike. I'm getting this bike." It really was like a scene in a movie when the character snaps and they're just having the best time.

I got it home about a week later and went for my next level of testing the following week for the licensing. I got my license, came home, jumped on my bike, went for a ride out into the bush just by myself, because I could.

There were so many birds. You could feel the rainforest humidity in the air. As I was breathing, I could smell and feel everything around me, and it was just completely exhilarating. I had ridden bikes plenty of times before this, but there was something about that first ride on my own bike that had me feeling like THIS is freedom. Because I did this for myself, I realized that I could wake up any day and decide: this is what I'm doing today.

It's interesting because I know it's a freedom that I always had, I just didn't know how to tap in and utilize it. It's so funny, because I always considered myself someone who would do whatever they wanted, but that wasn't actually the case.

I actively made a decision to do something with no one else considered but myself, and that was the moment when I recognized that I could unlock that power.

Life has been so freeing since buying my bike and obtaining my license. My relationship is better, my work life is better, my ability to set boundaries with my family is better.

I've even found myself more rooted in my identity as Aboriginal Australian woman. The Indigenous connection to spirituality is something that's amplified when you're in preserved native spaces. Riding takes me to these spaces in such connective ways.

Motorcycling also opened new ties to my magical practice that I hadn't even considered beforehand. Much of my childhood was marked by two driving forces that have naturally fallen into place for me as an adult—bikes, and witchcraft. Living a lifestyle that's deeply rooted in a connection to the land comes naturally down the line on my mother's side of the family thanks to our Indigenous/Aboriginal Australian heritage.

My earliest memories are imprinted with the lessons I've learned about Mother Earth and the beautiful gifts that She gives us if we take care of Her properly. From the other side of my family, I had a family member who practiced Wicca who would generously give me all manner of books and trinkets which opened my mind to the ways that magical practice can help to guide your way.

My grandfather also taught me how to read tarot cards. He was a seasoned veteran of the theater, so he used tarot more as a performative piece, but I was intrigued enough to find ways to tap into it further as a magical tool.

As a teen I found in some ways that I was struggling to find my place in the world of magic despite feeling such a connection to it. A lot of the resources out there tapped into more of Wiccan/Pagan/Northern sort of perspective on magic. The holistic elements made sense, but it doesn't translate across well in the Southern Hemisphere. Think about books and art depicting a crackling Yule log while I'm sweating my ass off in 100-degree weather with high-humidity, it just doesn't feel genuine at all.

As I got older, I started getting a little more defiant in my practice and doing my own thing while also starting to gather my own understanding that this is what witchcraft is all about. I slowly came to the realization that the influences that come from my mother (and her mother, who I unfortunately never had the privilege to meet) from the perspective of how Indigenous culture drives the understanding of your place in the world had a lot in common with these holistic elements of magical practice.

The animals and plants each hold their own totemic meanings, there is a strong belief in a spiritual realm (which is defined a little differently and referred to as "the Dreaming" in Indigenous Australian culture) and there is a shared emphasis on recognizing and celebrating the Earth's many seasonal changes throughout the year.

I realized I didn't need a book to tell me how to practice magic, I was already doing it in a way. I find it incredibly humbling and validating that in our family (at least in the Dharawal mob that our family comes from) it's not called witchcraft or magic, nor is it really treated as something different, it's just the way of life.

Getting out on my bike is my chance to truly get amongst the land in ways that allow me to appreciate it so much more than in a car. We're blessed with lots of twisty mountain roads in South-East Queensland, with most of them flanked by gorgeous flora.

If you go out on a ride in these areas, you'll be gifted with the sights of all sorts of bird life in the trees and other critters on the ground (but don't forget to scan your eyes over the side of the road for kangaroos—you do NOT wanna get into a collision with a 'roo!)

Personally, this has been one of the biggest pieces of my practice that I didn't realize was missing. To feel the wind against your body and smell the freshness of the air as you're cruising in the thick of the Earth is unlike anything else when it comes to how magic can be woven into everyday life.

It's an undeniable spiritual connection that I can feel in these moments, like I'm a part of something bigger when I'm out on my bike. The stories of Mother Earth in all Her beauty and brutality gain some visibility.

That's really the ethos that I weave into my practice: I'm equal to the tree, I'm not better than the tree, and I wholeheartedly believe that.

.⁺+

**Raegan, USA:** I started riding in October of 2020, although riding was something I had always been interested in. I never knew my biological grandfather, but the only stories I had ever heard about him were his adventures and involvement with a Biker Club.

One day he rolled through a small South Carolina town where he met my grandma and that's how my mother came to be. When I was a child, I was always curious about our family story, and I was always someone who had been drawn toward more masculine things. Motorcycles, in my mind as a kid, was one of those things.

It wasn't until my husband Sean and I started dating that we began talking about riding. We didn't have a lot of money our first few years of marriage, but we would go to the Harley dealership and sit on the bikes and daydream about it.

In 2020, we had a lot of life changes happening such as finally settling a lawsuit that was emotionally draining and leaving our home in Georgia for our next Army adventure. We decided to try to get pregnant and start our family. I was 27 and it was my golden year.

We had been trying for about 10 or 11 months to get pregnant, and at the time I was very into wellness and anything to do with nutrition and exercise. I was always an athletic person, but I realize now I was just reaching for anything that would get me pregnant. My mom was always super fertile, and I questioned why it was taking so long.

We finally got pregnant in May of 2020, and we were just overjoyed. It was such a beautiful time. I was super confident that I was doing all the right things—eating all the right things, meditating, sitting in the sun, taking vitamins, sleeping a lot. I was the happiest I had ever been. It felt like the right time. We went somewhere early in the pregnancy where they do only ultrasounds and we actually went twice because we were so excited to hear the heartbeat.

When we finally got to see the OB, they couldn't find the heartbeat anymore. I didn't believe him and what he was telling me. After a while, he brought in other technicians who also couldn't find the heartbeat. This was during Covid, so I was alone, and my husband was in the waiting room. I walked out to him in the waiting room, just completely sobbing.

They sent us downstairs in the hospital to get an internal ultrasound to confirm. We were in a panicked, devastated place of knowing but not knowing. There was a lot of messiness on the hospital's part on the wait time and confirming it. We found out that I was about 11 weeks along but the heartbeat probably stopped around 7 weeks, so my body hadn't registered that the pregnancy should've been over. We were devastated.

I had to do a lot of work with my therapist afterwards to work through the illusion of control that I had for myself—getting pregnant and letting go of pregnancy. All that stuff is completely out of my control. As someone who has gone through a lot of body trauma that is difficult to accept. It was painful and it's still difficult to accept.

Some months passed after that. We didn't know what to do or if we should try again. We were both emotionally broken up afterwards. At the time, Sean got promoted at work and suddenly, we were in a different place. On a random Saturday we went to a Harley dealership to look around and saw a Sportster on sale. We left but we started talking about just buying it.

After the miscarriage, Sean really wanted to do something for me that was empowering and positive. We ended up getting the bike. I learned to ride and then he got his own. The more I learned to ride, it helped me make peace with that transitional phase, not knowing what to do after the miscarriage was hard and feeling like I couldn't replace what I had lost.

After that, it didn't feel right to just try again but that left me in this weird space of feeling like I was floating. Something that felt natural and real to me was taken away.

The motorcycle was able to fill that space. It gave me something positive and fun and powerful to put that energy into. It also helped me feel like I was in control of my body and it's such a hard thing to describe to people who don't ride. The feeling of riding feels like flying and at a certain point everything melts away and it feels like you and your bike are one thing existing together.

It gave me an overwhelming sense of power and control. Although it was something that was outside of my body, it made me feel in control of my body in a positive way. It also really helped me move through the feeling of letting go. You can just release whatever you need to release, and the wind will take it away.

.⁺✦

**Sabrina, USA:** I was raised by my Japanese grandparents and in my culture, not many women have historically ridden motorcycles or had tattoos. We are seeing a progressive shift now in many ways with the increasing number of women riding and building awesome choppers, but I spent a lot of my youth saying, "I really want a motorcycle. We'll see what happens in the future."

When I got older, I ended up falling in love with someone when I lived in Los Angeles who had a Triumph Thruxton, and it was badass. My first time on a motorcycle was on the back of that bike and we did a road trip from Los Angeles to San Francisco. I remember loving the thrill.

When that relationship crumbled, I was heartbroken but the one thing I got from it was "I need to get my own bike. I can do this." It took me a few years to be able to get the funds, but I eventually bought a little cafe racer 200. I worked so hard on it but there was something wrong with the electrical. I trailered it to an all-women's moto event called Babes Ride Out and when I took it out for a ride, it died on the way to the gas station.

A friend of mine who was familiar with that specific kind of bike said it wasn't going to work, so I just got on the back of hers and we explored Joshua Tree National Park and had a blast. This was my first glimpse into the camaraderie and support that lives within the women's motorcycle community. I've always felt like an outsider to the outsiders but when I got into motorcycles is when I really found my people.

I eventually decided to get myself a Harley and it was a whole other feeling with the power and the rumble. I realized I could modify it and make it my own. I've had my bike Wanda for 8 years now and we've been through a lot together. I named her Wanda inspired by the song Fujiyama Mama by Wanda Jackson because I'm a Japanese woman on an American bike.

Having that bike makes me feel invincible. On a whim, I decided to move to New Orleans with nothing but my motorcycle and anything I could pack that would fit on it for the journey. Serendipitously, shortly after deciding to move I had watched the movie *Easy Rider* and knew it was meant to be!

Motorcycles make me feel like I am capable of anything, and I can start over and as long as I have my bike I'm gonna be okay. Nothing beats the feeling of working on my motorcycle, getting to know it better, hitting the road and meeting the most interesting people.

I often reflect on all the ways my grandmother would be proud of me today. When I was a little girl, she shared many stories about growing up in China before and during WW2 and how she navigated that time and her experiences immigrating here to the United States.

She was a survivor, and I know she would be so proud of all the ways I have carried on our ability to take what we could fit in a bag and go.

Motorcycles provide an opportunity for me to carry on the resourceful, resilient, and powerful magic within our lineage in unique and fulfilling ways, all while creating an opportunity for me to redefine what it means to be a Japanese woman and blaze my own path in this world.

⁺₊

**Francesca, Wales:** I've always wanted to ride motorcycles, it's part of our family history. My dad has been a big Harley fan his whole life. He grew up fixing bikes with his dad but sold his bike when I was born to support the family financially. Despite always wanting to learn and get a bike, one thing led to another—finance and time wise something always got in the way.

A few years ago, back in 2016, my dad finally managed to get his dream Harley Davidson. A black and chrome Fat Boy that he used his skills to customize. I absolutely loved being a pillion and going on rides with him. There was such a sense of freedom, like an adventure I had never experienced before.

There are amazing landscapes here in Wales where I live. You can go from the coast into the mountains in about 20 minutes, and the roads are just incredible. Twisting through forests, challenging hairpin bends with steep drop offs to the side and long, scenic highways.

I loved getting to experience Wales in that way. Whipping through the landscape with the roar of the bike around me cleared my mind and was pure joy and freedom.

Eventually, I grew tired of riding on the back, and I decided that I should finally get my own license. I had my first lesson booked for March of 2020 but then everything shut down because of the pandemic.

That was when life got very difficult for me. I work in healthcare and the pandemic was tough on everyone involved. I found a lot of it very traumatizing and scary. I felt unsafe every day. I have

OCD and suddenly all the lies it tells you were real and true. I couldn't cope.

I know everyone had their own experiences, and everyone struggled in different ways, but I was really affected by it in terms of my mental health. I ended up having a mental breakdown. I couldn't work, was too afraid to leave my house and I fell into a deep depression. I didn't want to be here anymore, and it was like that for a long time. Everything felt so out of my control, and I was frightened all the time.

My family supported me, I took medication. I went through lots of therapy. I think my spiritual practice really supported me quite a lot. As I got better, I reconnected with it by doing grounding rituals when I felt unsafe and remembering the power I have over my life and my own mind. I remembered that magic is possible.

I spent a long time quite unwell but eventually I started to feel better. I went back to work and began seeing my friends again. However, I still felt like there was more I needed to do to rebuild myself. I felt that revisiting my dream of riding a motorbike was the best way to do that.

Before this all happened, I did feel strong and empowered. I felt like that was taken away from me and I knew learning to ride was going to help me get back to who I was.

I was eventually able to take my beginners course and I passed my first licensing test. I got out and rode hundreds of miles, challenging myself on all the roads that scared me. It has helped my confidence and empowered me so much.

Riding through these landscapes, I get the same feeling that I did when I was on the back of my dad's bike, but now I'm in control. I get to immerse myself in the landscape in a completely different and unique way and it's very healing.

I can't really think of anything else that could empower you so much as being in relationship with this machine and having this adventure and freedom. I can leave my problems on the road behind me and ride away.

Motorbikes have made my life so much bigger too. I've met wonderful people—especially other women who ride. I've made friends and formed relationships that will last a lifetime. I've had so many incredible experiences that make life worth living, with many more to come.

It's macabre, but I have gone from wanting to die and not wanting to be here anymore to now feeling acutely aware of the dangers of riding motorcycles. I have a healthy level of fear, which reminds me every time I ride that I want to be here. I want to live, and riding a motorcycle is the most alive I've ever felt.

⁺⁺

**Rina, Costa Rica:** Riding motorcycles was random for me. Nobody in my family rides and I didn't plan to learn how to. I never pictured myself having one, but I always liked them. A few years ago, I saw two women on a Harley, and I thought they were so cool. My journey began when I moved out of the city and realized I needed transportation to take me to university.

I didn't want to take public transportation because the process itself is difficult and uncomfortable with a backpack and my books. My now ex-boyfriend suggested I ride a scooter. Scooters are very common here in Costa Rica. I thought to myself, "sure I can ride a scooter, but if I'm spending money on a scooter why not buy something that I really like?"

I started looking at motorcycles and found a 200cc bike at the shop and decided to buy it. I knew nothing about motorcycles and had no idea how to ride it. The man who sold it to me asked if I was going to ride it home and I said, "no I don't know how to ride it." He looked at me like I was crazy.

After I got the bike home, I taught myself how to ride using YouTube. Riding courses were too expensive, and I didn't know anyone who rode a motorcycle who could teach me. It was a difficult process, but I took baby steps and eventually got better and more comfortable.

My experience getting into motorcycles seemed random at the time, but looking back I realized it was exactly what I needed. During that time in my life, I was dealing with a brutal depression. I constantly had intrusive thoughts about dying and I didn't care about anything.

University was stressful, I had no money, and I didn't have anyone to help me with finances. I had to always look out for myself. Everything felt like it was too much. I wasn't living but only surviving at the time.

It wasn't until after I started riding when I noticed that I was feeling again. I no longer felt numb. Three months later, after learning how to ride, I began thinking about buying a bigger motorcycle. I decided to sell my first bike to buy the one I have now. It was a used bike but all the bikes I love are really old, so it was perfect.

We drove two hours to see the motorcycle and when we arrived, the owner turned the bike on, and I immediately fell in love with the sound. I took it for a test ride, and I knew it was my bike. I bought the motorcycle that same day. I felt so full of joy. I remember the day was beautiful. The sun was shining, and the roads were perfect.

A lot of amazing things have happened since I got that motorcycle. I've met amazing friends and community, I've learned how to work on bikes, and I hope to someday build my dream chopper.

I'm so thankful to have found *my thing*. I've never had anything in my life that felt like it was mine. I've never had anything in my life that I enjoyed so much. Riding motorcycles helped me get out of that horrible black hole I was stuck in, and I'm just so thankful to be here.

.⁺✦

**Gabrielle, USA:** My earliest memory of motorcycles traces back to a trip to California with my mom and stepdad. I don't recall exactly where we were staying, but I vividly remember the Harley parked there. My stepdad said, "I'm gonna take you on a motorcycle ride," and we cruised through streets lined with palm trees, the ocean shimmering in the distance.

Something magical awakened inside me that day. From that moment, motorcycles captivated me, their pull was undeniable.

In junior high, I had a friend with dirt bikes who would zip around his yard and take me along for the ride. Watching him, I knew deep down I needed a dirt bike of my own. We didn't have much money—we were living in a trailer park—but my mom scraped together enough to buy me an old 1990s Honda.

It didn't even run, and while my stepdad promised to fix it, he never did. The bike sat untouched under the carport. After my mom's divorce, the bike disappeared, but my fascination with motorcycles stayed.

By high school, I was glued to the window every time I heard the roar of a motorcycle. Occasionally, I'd hop on the back of my boyfriends' bikes, but even then, I knew I wanted more. I didn't want to be a passenger; I wanted to ride.

I learned how to ride on a battered old Harley. It was too big, too heavy, and far from ideal for a beginner. The first time I took it out, I rode to a nearby cul-de-sac but didn't know how to turn. I tipped over, and the bike landed on my ankle.

Somehow, through adrenaline or sheer determination, I managed to lift the bike on my own. That spill landed me in the ER with a sprained ankle and bruises. Learning to ride was put on pause, and soon life shifted.

At 20, I was pregnant with my son Jaden. My dreams of riding took a backseat as I focused on motherhood. Yet, every spring when the motorcycles emerged, I felt a familiar yearning. But the doubts crept in. Society tells moms, "You can't do that. It's dangerous. What if something happens to you?" For years, I bought into that narrative. I told myself, "That'll never be me. I'm a mom now."

Then, in my mid-30s, just before the pandemic, a health scare forced me to confront my mortality. Specialists, scans, and MRIs had me terrified. For the first time, I realized how much of my life I'd spent neglecting myself.

I was so consumed by motherhood that I didn't know who I was outside of it. Raising five kids—my three biological children and two stepsons—left no room for me. Something inside snapped, and I decided, "I'm going to learn to ride."

It wasn't an easy decision. My ex-husband wasn't supportive at first, but I made it clear it wasn't up for discussion. For once, I wasn't asking for permission. I signed up for a class in September 2020. It was during COVID, so we wore masks under helmets, adding to the surreal feeling of the experience. I was one of only three women, surrounded mostly by men. It was exhilarating and terrifying.

After the first day, I was physically and emotionally drained. The next morning, I broke down crying, convinced I couldn't go back. I even tried convincing myself I was sick, but I'd come too far to quit. Jaden was my biggest cheerleader. He gave me a pep talk. He said, "Mom, you've got this. You're better at this than you think." Bolstered by his words, I returned to class, and I passed.

By then, I already owned my dream bike, a 2006 CBR 600 RR. I'd bought it two months earlier, even though I couldn't ride it yet. It sat in the garage, waiting, as I familiarized myself with it. Once I had my endorsement, I started practicing in my neighborhood. Every ride was a challenge. I stalled at stop signs, struggled with hill starts, but I refused to give up.

Eventually, I found myself drawn to cruisers. I fell in love with Indian motorcycles and bought a Scout Bobber. A year later, I became an Indian Motorcycle brand ambassador, a dream I never imagined possible.

Riding gave me confidence, fearlessness, and a deep connection to myself. It's something I now share with other women, encouraging them to embrace their individuality. Society often frames self-prioritization as selfish, especially for mothers, but I've learned that having something just for you makes you better in every role you play.

Looking back, the journey was anything but smooth. Between 2021 and 2022, I went through a divorce, returned to school, pursued a new career after a decade as a stay-at-home mom, and fully immersed myself in the world of motorcycles. It was a whirlwind, but it taught me resilience.

Motorcycles brought me freedom, community, and identity. They didn't just change my life; they helped me find myself. For the first time, I felt like Gabrielle—not just a mom, wife, or friend, but a woman with her own passions and purpose.

**Nina, Norway:** There's always been a part of me that knew I was meant to ride motorcycles. The spark was there, even though I didn't grow up in a world of bikes. We lived in a rural area where the neighbors had motorcycles on their farm, but there was enough of an age gap between them and me and my brother that we never really bonded over it. Still, the idea of motorcycles stirred something inside me.

My parents had bikes back in the mid-80s, but they sold them after my younger brother was born. I didn't grow up on the back of a bike, but I did grow up in a household where you fixed things yourself. We lived on an old farm. We didn't have animals, but we farmed the land and maintained the property.

I remember waking up to the sound of my parents telling us, "It's your turn—put your boots on." We'd head outside to round up the sheep that had wandered on to our land. I have vague memories of handing my dad tools while he fixed the tractor. If something was broken, we fixed it. Living in the countryside you don't just replace things, but you learn to be resourceful.

As an adult, a series of experiences brought me to a turning point—I knew it was time to do something just for me. I realized it was finally time to make one of my longtime dreams a reality: learning to ride. By 2017, just before my 28th birthday, I made the decision to get my motorcycle license.

The season was winding down, but I managed to power through the last test before winter set in. I had just started my career, so my bike budget was tight. Still, I knew I had to make it happen.

With student loans and all the usual adult responsibilities, I thrifted what I could, put the rest on a credit card, and lived off ramen noodles for a while. True to my "fix it yourself" mentality, I bought a bike that wouldn't start. It was the perfect fit, but it needed work. I got it halfway running, but more often than not, I had to push it around the block in full leathers, sweating in my helmet, just to get it going.

At first, I didn't know many people my age who were into riding. A couple of older guys—one in his 50s, another in his 80s—took me under their wing and offered guidance. They were incredibly kind and welcoming, and I'm grateful for their support.

Still, their riding style was rougher than I preferred, and they often led with a lot of ego. Over time, I realized I needed to create something of my own: a community of women who shared my passion for motorcycles.

I noticed that women often rode either with male friends or alone, and there was a clear gap in the female riding community. While a few clubs existed, many were made up of women of an older generation who had fought hard to pave the way for women like me to ride freely.

I'm deeply grateful for their courage and resilience, and it inspired me to create a different kind of space, one where women could thrive together on two wheels without having to fight so hard to claim their place in the community.

I took a leap and joined an international riding event called Women Riders World Relay, which brought women together from all corners of the world. After it passed through Norway, I was left wondering, "What's next?" I scrolled through the event page and messaged women who had attended, inviting them to meet for coffee.

That simple act grew into a movement. Our group kept expanding as we met more women who shared our love for motorcycles.

Eventually, we started a festival here in Norway—the Cats on Wheels Women's Motorcycle Festival. It became our way of creating space for female makers, builders, and riders to showcase their work, share knowledge, and bond over everything related to bikes.

Looking back, I realize it was never just about learning to ride. It was about uncovering the wild, unstoppable force that lives inside all of us.

The motorcycles we ride don't just carry us from place to place; they are symbols of freedom and empowerment.

They guide us forward and remind us that the power we hold as women is limitless. With every ride, we prove it.

# Rest Area #5

Welcome to your fifth Rest Area. You've officially explored the full road map of the Biker Witch path. Remember, this map is entirely yours. You can revisit spaces that stood out, sit with the emotions or thoughts that arose, and return to any activities that continue to call to you.

Here, you'll take a moment to reflect on all the experiences, challenges, and awakenings that brought you here. Your own initiatory moments have pulled you into a life of magic, and I'm so glad to be riding it with you.

Answer the next few questions in your journal at your own pace, allowing yourself to exhale and absorb the journey so far. When you feel ready, we'll prepare for the next leg of the ride.

**Tools You'll Need**

- A journal
- A writing utensil

1. CAN YOU DESCRIBE A PIVOTAL INITIATORY EXPERIENCE
THAT TRANSFORMED YOUR UNDERSTANDING OF YOURSELF AND
YOUR PLACE IN THE WORLD?

2. WHAT ANCESTRAL OR CULTURAL STORIES RESONATE WITH
YOU AS YOU EXPLORE YOUR IDENTITY AS A BIKER WITCH?
HOW DO THESE STORIES INFORM YOUR PERSONAL NARRATIVE?

3. IN WHAT WAYS HAS EMBRACING WITCHCRAFT OR
MOTORCYCLING ALLOWED YOU TO RECLAIM AUTONOMY,
PERSONAL POWER, OR SELF-EXPRESSION?

4. WHAT FORCES OR MOMENTS PULLED YOU ONTO THIS PATH,
EVEN IF UNEXPECTEDLY OR UNWILLINGLY?

5. HOW DO YOU RELATE TO THE PARADOX OF DEATH AS
REBIRTH IN YOUR OWN JOURNEY OF TRANSFORMATION?

6. WHAT FEARS OR OLD BELIEFS DID YOU HAVE TO RELEASE TO STEP FULLY INTO YOUR BIKER WITCH IDENTITY?

7. HOW HAVE MOMENTS OF DARKNESS OR STRUGGLE DEEPENED YOUR CONNECTION TO THE GREAT MOTHER OR YOUR SPIRIT ALLIES?

8. IN WHAT WAYS DO YOU FEEL INITIATION IS ONGOING RATHER THAN A SINGLE EVENT?

9. HOW DO YOU HONOR AND HOLD SPACE FOR VULNERABILITY AS A SOURCE OF STRENGTH IN YOUR JOURNEY?

10. WHAT DOES FREEDOM MEAN TO YOU NOW, COMPARED TO BEFORE YOUR INITIATION EXPERIENCE?

# GETTING READY

# Rubber Meets the Road

It's a lot to take in, isn't it, Biker Witch? We've covered a lot of ground together. Now it's time to gear up and get ready for the ride ahead. Your homecoming to the Great Mother may have marked the end of one life, but it's only the beginning of the one unfolding before you now.

She was the one who stirred the longing. She called you to the edge, pulled you across the threshold from who you were into the deeper mysteries of who you truly are. Having nurtured you through the threshold, She now sends you on your way to move with and learn from your spirit kin.

The spirits are our guides and confidants. They are the weavers, the protectors, and the keepers of the flame. They guard the spark She lit within. Through our relationships with them, we remain rooted within Her.

This is the moment when remembering becomes integration—when everything you've touched, felt, and known begins to shape the way you live. This is where the rubber meets the road, and it all begins with *you*.

Let's revisit our definition of a witch:

**Someone who utilizes *the art of relationship* to connect with spirits and allows themselves to be transformed by the insight and guidance they receive.**

Spirits do more than enhance your magic. They offer their own living intelligence, expanding what is already alive and aware within you. Through this reciprocal bond, your power grows more potent and whole.

Before you can enter into relationship with them, you must face a fundamental truth: your ability to engage with and embrace the world around you depends on how deeply you are willing to turn inward and tend to the world within.

To *allow* yourself to be transformed by spirits, you must cultivate a relationship with yourself based on openness to growth, a readiness to evolve, and a steady commitment to meet your inner landscape with honesty. This turning inward prepares us for the alchemical process of **dynamic becoming**.

Dynamic becoming is the ongoing journey of transformation. It's the conscious embrace of life's constant flux and the understanding that change is not only inevitable but essential.

The Great Mother may have catalyzed your first major transformation, pulling you through surrender onto this path, but that initial pull was only the beginning. Now the work is yours.

You must *choose* to continue transforming, to notice when the circumstances of your life feel out of alignment with the web of life, and to take the steps needed to realign yourself. You become the one who actively invites growth and creates openings for change.

Your relationships with spirits will continue to guide, challenge, and push you beyond who you once were. Remaining receptive to their insight is essential for ongoing transformation.

In a world shaped by centuries of patriarchy, where women have been told who they are and who they should be, dynamic becoming is a radical rebellion. Choosing to evolve beyond inherited stories is a powerful act of defiance.

This defiance doesn't just change you; it reverberates outward. Your journey of self-discovery becomes inseparable from your witchcraft. It fuels your magic, and your healing and growth become threads in the larger web of life, strengthening the relationships that bind us to each other.

If I'm being completely honest, much of what we learn about witchcraft today overlooks this web of life, and even the modern witchcraft community hasn't fully escaped patriarchal values. Too frequently, it perpetuates cycles of seeking personal "power" defined by domination, wealth, and capitalist ideals.

While individual empowerment has its place on a spiritual path, it can come at the cost of our collective well-being, often disregarding the impact of our actions on other beings. This focus on hyper-individualism undermines our potential for genuine liberation as a shared movement toward life beyond patriarchy.

Robin Artisson captures the essence of modern spirituality quite potently in *The Clovenstone Workings: A Manual of Early Modern Witchcraft*:

> We must exercise caution when we turn towards the confluence of "self" for special insights, because our human world is obsessed—entirely—by a foolish devotion to an invented notion, a false consciousness, of a hyper-individual *self-construct*. We live in a *self*-ish world, in which idealized notions of self are elevated to positions of psychological or social supremacy. Long gone are the days when the human self was shaped, known, and nurtured primarily in *relation to an intimate community*—a communal and relational situation in which selves could share with others, receive and co-create healthy support and healthy outcomes in ordinary circumstances (48).

We often see this obsession with the "self" reflected in the language we encounter in pop culture when discussing witchcraft. Terms like the vague "universe" or "manifesting" offer no real framework for relationship.

Instead, they center the individual human experience, casting us as the architects of our own lives with no deeper rooting beyond our perceived ability to manipulate the powers of the world for personal gain. This ultimately distorts our understanding of who we are and where we stand within the web of life, distancing us further from Her.

Our magic as Biker Witches isn't about striving to be the "best version" of ourselves, accumulating wealth, or gaining power in the human world. It's not about "fixing" ourselves to reach some ultimate enlightened state, nor about positioning ourselves as saviors of humanity.

Instead, our path calls us to inhabit a self that is wild, porous, and in ongoing conversation with the world around us. We become someone who is receptive, responsive, and open to integrating the insights we receive from spirits in every unfolding moment.

We become a vessel through which magic flows, not to lift us above, but to root us deeper into Her. Like a plant drawing strength from the earth, we're nourished by what the spirits share, opening ourselves to act as conduits for Her and restoring the balance of power not only within ourselves but also across the wider ecosystem to which we belong.

Before this process can bloom, many of us will first require a clearing, an upheaval of what once settled within us to help us survive. It involves naming and unlearning the patriarchal patterns that still live within us so we can uproot them, make space for something new to grow, and tend that space with courage.

We've already named that the ride itself will be our ritual, a way to release the burdens of our foremothers and our own. However, this conditioning runs deep, and every transformation we undergo continuously reveals old layers to be shed, some we didn't even know were there.

In our efforts to endure patriarchy and make sense of this world, many of us have clung to patterns of self-preservation, lived within our wounds, or defined ourselves by the stories of what has happened to us rather than claiming the role of the one holding the pen.

Though the wounds inflicted by patriarchy are not our fault—we've been dealt a shit hand—we do have a say in how we play the cards. We can take ownership of our lives by recognizing the ways we may have unconsciously contributed to our own wounding.

We can notice how we hold on to familiar patterns, those that once protected us but now keep us living within old stories and inhibiting the transformations we now long for.

Taking ownership of our lives can feel daunting, scary, or even shameful as we reckon with the ways we've turned away from it. It is in summoning the courage to take that first step, really looking in the mirror, seeing who is looking back, and acknowledging who has been writing our story, that true transformation begins.

In these moments of facing ourselves despite fear or discomfort, we learn to trust ourselves. We start to build an honest, moment-to-moment relationship with who we are. This is where we learn to "be where we really are," as Sadee Whip says in *Savage Awakening: Initiatory Paths of the Dragon Mother:*

> Being where you really are is to sit with the truth of yourself **as you are** in any particular moment—with the judgment, shame, the pain, the fragility—all *without resigning yourself to what you find and without the urge to fix it in the moment it is experienced* (28).

Being truly present with ourselves means facing our complexities without the impulse to escape, numb, or resist what's before us. When we face ourselves with unwavering honesty, we begin to understand where we've been, who we are, and what has shaped us up until now.

As judgment and pain shift into curiosity, we're able to hold ourselves with greater skill and understanding, staying open to possibility rather than retreating into shame.

With curiosity now as your compass, take a moment to look at the patterns you may have carried into your spiritual journey so far. How might your practice have, at times, served as a crutch that upholds patriarchal conditioning, keeping you hardened and striving to fix or perfect yourself?

Have you been chasing an idealized version of yourself that always feels just out of reach? Does each challenge you overcome seem to reveal another, arriving from a different angle?

Have you found yourself using your practice to constantly try to "fix" what feels broken inside, endlessly chasing something that remains beyond your grasp?

It's okay if your answers are yes. It's okay if you don't know yet. These questions aren't meant to offer easy answers but to invite you to consider where you may have been caught in a one-sided conversation with only the parts of yourself you've been taught to judge, silence, or improve—a conversation shaped by systems that prize control, perfection, and independence over vulnerability, relationship, and surrender.

When our healing remains stagnant and solitary, we cut ourselves off from the forces of transformation. We are held in place by the very narratives we hoped to escape, reinforcing the same patriarchal ideals we long to dismantle.

This is why we soften into the process of becoming. Because the truth is that our becoming never ends. It's a lived rhythm, a way of being that moves in harmony with what is.

Becoming honors that we are cyclical beings of the earth, ever-responsive to the shifting forces within us and around us. We are always listening, receiving, integrating, unraveling, returning, and we are always becoming again.

Just as your altar shifts with the seasons and the phases of your life, so do you. Letting go of parts of yourself becomes just as essential as fully embracing who you are in each moment, freed from the weight of old conditioning and patterns that no longer support your evolutions.

This journey also calls us to take a step further into our own lives by embracing our becoming as consistent spiritual maintenance—regular check-ins on the fluidity and adaptability of our path.

Even the identities, practices, or communities that once opened us to connection and curiosity can begin to solidify into fixed definitions, closing us off to relationships without us even realizing it.

It's incredibly human to try to protect ourselves from uncertainty or to find our belonging in a world shaped by patriarchal norms. After generations of fighting so hard just to survive, it's no wonder we seek safety through certainty, even if that means shrinking ourselves or clinging to what once worked.

For instance, if you've identified as a witch throughout your life, has your practice become a way to define yourself in a fixed and unchanging way?

Have you adopted a particular type of witchcraft as a permanent identity, using it as a shield against a world that might not fully understand you?

Have you relied on this label to fit into a certain mold, focusing on rituals, spells, and practices that reinforce certainty about who you are rather than inviting the unknown?

Similarly, as a biker, has your motorcycle become a protective barrier between you and the deeper, more vulnerable journey of self-discovery? Has it been a way to push back against societal pressures while also holding on to a version of yourself that feels safer, easier, or more accepted?

While these fixed states may offer a sense of security, as if we're planting a flag and declaring who we are, true belonging doesn't come from rigid boundaries or a set and unchangeable sense of self. These identities and passions may have given us strength, and even survival, but they can also tether us to limited versions of who we believe we must be.

Only by embracing fluidity and openness to becoming can we begin to feel what it's like to truly belong to Her. This is the heart of dynamic becoming. It asks us to release control without losing sovereignty, to soften without disappearing, and to move with the transformative forces that shape us rather than resist them.

## Becoming

You've committed to the path of transformation. You've chosen to stay fluid, to check in with yourself regularly, and to integrate the insight the spirits offer along the way. This is no small commitment.

It means showing up consistently, even when the changes are subtle or hard to recognize. Sometimes, even with dedicated practice, it can be difficult to notice the shifts unfolding within us in real time.

As Artisson writes in *The Clovenstone Workings: A Manual of Early Modern Witchcraft*:

> Being what you are, with the sorts of storytelling minds we have, we don't often pay attention to our changing selves. Our stories tend to be stories of stability, of changing unpredictability, of achievement, or of the nostalgia of the past; we change and yet we don't notice our own changes. What we often notice happening in others is *certainly* happening in us, but since we are perceptually with ourselves every day, every hour, every moment, it's hard to see all that we have gradually become, and what we are becoming (49).

Our close proximity to our own lives can make it difficult to perceive our transformations as they happen. We may not always recognize when our spiritual questions have shifted or when new insights have arrived through our spirit allies.

As Biker Witches, we are uniquely prepared for this challenge. Our ritualized ride will also serve as a container for shaping and witnessing our own becoming.

Each ride creates a ritual arc that invites us to notice what emerges before we set out, during the journey, and after we return. This rhythm naturally weaves the art of relationship into our lives and teaches us to welcome change as it comes.

We begin with preparation, grounding into intention and presence, and noticing what thoughts or emotions arise as we make our asks to the spirits and leave offerings at the altar.

Then we ride, allowing our motorcycle companions to carry us through the world and dissolve the illusion of separation. On the road, time softens. The wind reorients our bodies and sharpens our senses.

The transformations we asked for become something we can feel. We begin to release the stories that once confined us, the inherited beliefs about who we should be or how we must act. We stop striving for perfection and instead meet life as it truly is.

As we open to the world, the world opens with us. We no longer demand that everything make sense, and the beings we encounter along the road become free to exist as they are. The spirits of place begin to sense that we've created space for genuine connection, and we find somewhere to pull over and connect with them.

We share offerings of gratitude and, in return, they may begin to share more about who they are. Sometimes they give us answers to our questions, and other times they simply give us the precious feeling of being witnessed.

This process helps us feel our place within the larger story. Personhood becomes no longer only a human trait; it becomes a felt essence, no more wise, worthy, or real than the spirits of our motorcycles, the lands we traverse, or the flowers we stop to smell along the way.

This way of relating invites recognition between beings, drawing us into a mutual exchange of offering, receiving, and restoring power within the web of life.

As the day turns and the journey begins to close, the energy of motion settles into the quiet of return. When we arrive back at the stillness of our home, we return once more to our altar. We enter reflection. We speak our insights aloud, jot them down in journals, name what changed us, and ask our spirit guides for a dream to carry our inquiry further.

This is how we document the movement of our becoming in real time. By ritualizing the ride, we begin to understand that our becoming is not only our own. It belongs to the forest that listens in silence, the crow watching with knowing eyes from the fencepost, and the rocks basking warmly in the sun.

Every moment leaves a mark, bringing a new knowing, a shift in perspective, a felt connection to everything around us. Over time, we stop feeling the need to define ourselves so tightly.

Instead, we tune into the natural rhythms unfolding all around us: the waxing and waning of the moon, the turning of the seasons, the migrations of animals, the shifting skies overhead, and the ever-changing landscapes beneath our tires.

We grow more aware of how these cycles pulse through our own existence, guiding our daily lives and shaping how we move through the world.

As the Earth spins, rivers carve their paths, and trees shed their leaves in cycles of death and renewal, we recognize how we too move through phases of becoming, shedding, and growing. The more we see ourselves as part of this rhythm, the more easily we allow ourselves to transform within it.

When we embrace transformation as an ongoing process, our ability to hold ourselves in our full humanity grows. We learn to hold our pain, grief, and trauma with compassion.

Self-compassion carries us beyond survival, shifting us from only being able to passively receive what our spirit allies share into actively participating in these relationships as an act of **devotion.**

We honor them not by trying to fix ourselves, but by refusing to shrink into the roles the world has handed us. We honor them by choosing to live fully and boldly in defiance of everything that once tried to silence and erase them from our lives.

In return, they offer us something rare: the freedom to stop treating ourselves like a project, to stop performing, and to let go of identities and stories that no longer fit.

From that freedom, we become one with life itself, moving in a continual flow of reciprocity. Over time, our lives and our practice become the ultimate expression of **love.**

We allow ourselves to be transformed by the many beings we cherish while choosing to shape the world with all the love we have to give in return.

# Rest Area #6

Welcome to your sixth Rest Area. You are nearing the close of these Rest Area activities, and with it, you are invited to pause and reflect on the journey of your own becoming.

This is a space to soften, to listen, and to honor how far you've come. Every insight you've uncovered, and will continue uncovering, is part of the transformations already unfolding within you.

## Tools You'll Need

- A journal
- A writing utensil

1. WHAT PARTS OF YOURSELF ARE CURRENTLY BEING RESHAPED BY THE ROAD YOU'RE TRAVELING?

2. IN WHAT WAYS ARE YOU RESISTING CHANGE, EVEN WHEN YOU KNOW IT'S NECESSARY FOR YOUR EVOLUTION?

3. WHAT LANDSCAPES, INTERNAL OR EXTERNAL, ARE CALLING YOU TO SLOW DOWN AND LISTEN MORE DEEPLY?

4. WHEN THE ROAD GETS ROUGH, WHO OR WHAT DO YOU TURN TO FOR GUIDANCE AND GROUNDING?

5. WHAT OUTDATED BELIEFS, NARRATIVES, OR ROLES ARE YOU READY TO RELEASE TODAY?

6. HOW DO YOU EXPERIENCE BELONGING AS A MOVING, LIVING EXPERIENCE RATHER THAN A STATIC PLACE?

7. WHERE IN YOUR LIFE ARE YOU WAITING FOR CONDITIONS TO BE "PERFECT" BEFORE YOU MOVE FORWARD?

8. WHAT IS ONE SMALL, TANGIBLE WAY YOU CAN HONOR YOUR BECOMING TODAY?

9. HOW CAN YOU CREATE SPACE IN YOUR DAILY LIFE TO WITNESS AND DOCUMENT YOUR TRANSFORMATIONS?

10. WHO DO YOU FEEL CALLED TO OFFER GRATITUDE OR OFFERINGS TO IN YOUR RITUAL PRACTICE RIGHT NOW?

# THE TWO WHEELS

The further along you ride on this mystical path, the more unrecognizable your life will become. Slowly at first, then all at once. The world around you won't just appear to be more beautiful, it will begin to share that beauty with you. What once felt one-sided will begin to relate and respond to you.

The offerings you leave at your altar or along the roadside will open new doors to wisdom. Roads you've ridden many times will reveal new stories. Dreams from spirits will guide you, and even the air will move differently around you.

This kind of vision is a gift, but at first, it can feel like a burden. As old frameworks crumble and your perception of the world shifts, you might feel like you're riding through a landscape no one else can name. You may want to share your feelings, insights, or discoveries with friends and family, but for many reasons, you can't.

Maybe it's because you already know they wouldn't understand, or maybe it's because putting yourself in such a vulnerable position of sharing would force you back into an outdated, smaller version of yourself that you've already evolved to outgrow.

Either way, in the early stretch of this new life, it might feel like it would be easier to live it completely alone, to believe that loneliness is the price one must pay as a witch.

But just because you're feeling alone doesn't mean that you are. That aching sense of distance isn't a true separation. More often, it's the very real tension marking the moment you realize that saying goodbye to a past life might also mean shifting how you show up in your relationships with the people who were part of it.

As one door closes behind you, shaped by familiar routines, shared worldviews, and the comfort of being understood, another opens. On the other side are invitations into new relationships, many of which are not sent by humans at all.

They might arrive on wings or padded feet, inhabit green bodies reaching toward the sun, emerge from stone and soil, or reveal themselves as entirely unseen.

You might feel a sudden urge to abandon your human life the moment you accept these invitations, but it is essential that you keep a steady foothold in the human world.

Because no matter how far we travel into mystery, which spirits we commune with, or what truths we uncover, we remain human—and our magic is not separate from that humanity. It is the extension of it.

Becoming a witch doesn't mean turning away from other humans. It means that the center of gravity in how you relate to them begins to shift. Even if you speak less, hold more, or carry truths others may never fully understand, your presence in your human community still matters.

The truth about belonging to Her is that the transformations we undergo are never just for us. They are meant to move through us, carried back into the web of life, and that web includes other humans.

When entire communities were colonized and humans were separated from the spirits long ago, the systems of patriarchy took hold, enforcing hierarchical and harmful ways to isolate us from the web of life.

Now, the insight we receive from spirits makes us collaborators and conduits for the restoration they long to see. These transformations take hold in us and extend beyond our own healing.

They move through our bodies, our choices, and our power, reaching the systems that have disconnected humans from each other and from the Earth.

We are being asked to carry what we learn with humility, to stay teachable, to remain malleable, and to listen. We are asked to become the embodied expression of their wisdom, helping to return balance to the world.

Our lives as witches are shaped by unseen forces and made visible through the everyday acts that keep us tethered to life itself, even if no one else sees the work we do or understands why.

## The Wheels of Witchcraft

As we begin to re-enter the human world with our gifts, a new kind of initiation begins. For many of us, the thought of bringing what we've learned back into human communities can activate deep wounds.

Giving up the comfort of being understood in a world shaped by patriarchal norms, while still being expected to remain connected to people who have harmed or dismissed one another for generations, can feel impossible. It can stir grief, anger, or hesitation.

We might ask why we should offer our magic to those committed to misunderstanding us, or why humanity deserves these gifts when all we've been taught is to hide, suppress, or fear them.

We might question whether it's our responsibility to tend to humans, and whether we haven't already given enough. These questions carry real weight. They don't arise solely from fear or doubt, but from lived experience.

Many of us carry wounds inflicted by other humans. We remember moments of misplaced trust, when we became entangled in dynamics that drained us. We recall being exiled from family, or watching friendships unravel when we could no longer remain silent.

Often, these wounds came not from failure or shying away from connection, but from our willingness to fully embody the roles we were taught to uphold in communities shaped by patriarchal values.

We gave without limit. We stayed too long. We quieted our needs to keep the peace. We believed love meant endurance. We thought loyalty meant swallowing our truth. We mistook boundaries for betrayal. We lost pieces of ourselves.

Beneath these personal stories lies an ancestral ache. Generations before us had their gifts silenced, punished, and pathologized. They survived at the edge of belonging. They were cast out, ridiculed, and erased.

In this light, it's no wonder that part of us wants to keep our magic for ourselves—to use it to rest, to thrive, and finally to feel safe. The thought of tending to human communities as a spiritual task can stir a reactionary desire to break away.

We might see the freedom we long for not as connection, but as detachment. Not as relationship, but as the absence of responsibility. We might imagine our spiritual path as escape, not as magic in service.

But here lies the paradox: we will never experience real freedom without embracing our accountability to others.

Without accountability, freedom becomes isolation. It leaves us passive, disconnected, and vulnerable to the very patriarchal forces we are trying to resist.

Without freedom, our accountability to others becomes a burden. It breeds resentment and leaves us feeling bound.

Only through the balance of **freedom** and **accountability** can we wield our magic in ways that usher a collective, revolutionary return to Her.

**These are the wheels of witchcraft.**

Like two wheels beneath us on a motorcycle, freedom and accountability move us forward together. One cannot carry us without the other. Together, they keep us steady, in motion, upright, and able to go the distance.

When we ride on both of these wheels, our questions begin to shift. They no longer ask whether we should withhold our magic from others, but what becomes possible when we hold it in protective care without retreating into isolation.

What can unfold when we keep our energy safe and our hearts open? How can we embrace our craft as a path that reminds us why we're here, fuels us to keep going, and holds us steady in our humanity even when the way forward feels uncertain?

The answers to these questions begin to emerge when we do the work of reframing what it means to be in relationship and redefining what it looks like to be part of our community in ways that uphold this balance on both wheels.

For generations, the roles we've held—as grandmothers, great-grandmothers, mothers, sisters, daughters, aunts, cousins, and friends—have not been without their challenges.

Within patriarchy, our roles in the ecosystem were distorted. Care became an obligation felt by women only. Connection was twisted into control. The vital work of tending was stripped of reciprocity and repackaged as duty.

In this climate, our fullest expression was stifled, our energy drained, and our labor co-opted to uphold systems that would rather consume and commodify us than care for us.

But the problem was never the roles themselves; it was the values that shaped and limited how we were allowed to embody them. Roles that once carried deep meaning were hollowed out and turned into tools to keep us compliant.

Many of the relationships we've endured in our own lives were formed within this framework. Beneath these wounds, though, something instinctive has survived.

Maybe you've felt it—the quiet pride in being the one who holds the center, who is willing to fight for what is meaningful, who brings new realities to life, who builds and nourishes community.

Even in a world that tried to diminish you, you recognized the importance of nurturing, protecting, creating, and keeping stories and kinship alive. There is no shame in that. There never was.

These roles, in their original form, carried the inherent power of the Great Mother. How else could these systems turn our strengths against us if not by distorting them with half-truths?

Instead of discarding these roles, we reclaim them. We restore them by learning how our foremothers participated within their communities before colonization, reclaiming both the ability and desire to care for ourselves and each other.

By doing so, we embrace the human community as part of the web of life while naming the truth that harmful systems have pushed us out of alignment with it.

We choose not to separate ourselves from humanity, but to help bring it back into right relationship within the ecosystem.

True freedom comes not from cutting ourselves off from responsibility, but from redefining what responsibility actually means and how we enact it.

## Redistribution

Redefining responsibility as a witch within your community quickly reveals how much oppressive systems have disrupted what was once reciprocal and balanced. This disruption means your fellow humans can't always show up for you in the ways you show up for them.

The same histories of colonialism that fractured the roles you now seek to reclaim also created uneven access to the resources necessary for collective reclamation and healing.

Because of these systems, some of us move through the world with an inherited proximity to safety, comfort, and power within patriarchy.

This proximity often reflects the ideals of the colonial empire: whiteness, wealth, able-bodiedness, heterosexuality, and being cisgender. These are not identities in themselves, but traces of a *system* that benefits some at the cost of many.

Navigating these systems is complicated. Complicity isn't always a reflection of privilege alone. Some of us who don't fall into these categories still pursue closeness to power within patriarchy because we've learned it's the only path to safety, success, or survival. Sometimes this comes from the longing to be safe in a world that makes it dangerous to remain fully ourselves.

Many of us became fluent in the language of power to avoid being dominated. We aligned with systems that harmed others, hoping they might spare us. We traded parts of ourselves to move closer to protection, even when it meant distancing from our people, our cultures, and our truths. This too is a form of loss that warrants both grieving and reclamation.

Acknowledging where we land within these systems allows us to see where and how we can bring our magic back into the ecosystem. Some of us were born in places where sunlight was abundant. Others have spent lifetimes in the shade. Those born into shadow often learned to push past others to find warmth, sometimes at the expense of connection.

No matter how we arrive at this moment, those of us who have grown into trees with wide canopies and deep roots are being called to nourish the forest around us. This is living in integrity with the Earth, the spirits, and our communities. This is how life sustains itself.

Understanding these uneven terrains is essential for our revolutionary work as witches. It helps us see the humanity in others and recognize that, for some, the burden of survival consumes the energy that might otherwise nurture connection.

Not everyone can show up in reciprocal ways because they're already depleted.

For those of us who inherit or occupy positions of relative privilege, there is a deeper responsibility to offset this imbalance and use our resources in service of repair. This asks us to share comforts and powers that were never meant to be ours alone. We do this not out of guilt or shame, but because our collective well-being depends on it.

As we navigate relationships within our communities, discernment is essential. Not everyone will be safe or ready to meet us in the kind of community we long for. Instead, we focus on finding our coven, our chosen kin, our trusted people.

We build relationships rooted in mutual care. We nurture the relational wisdom we're rediscovering and reclaiming, while also holding space for a broader love of humanity. This kind of love doesn't require exhausting ourselves trying to earn connection where it cannot yet exist. Embracing the collective doesn't mean abandoning discernment or putting ourselves in unsafe positions.

The spirits offer support in the face of this complexity. They help us remember who we are beneath what we were taught to become. They pour into us until we overflow, resourcing us to redistribute what we carry. They show up for us when reciprocity is impossible. They remind us that care must remain rooted in compassion, patience, and an unwavering love for life, even when it's messy or unreturned.

In the human world, this care looks like filling gaps where systems fail our communities. It means giving grace where we may once have given judgment. It means building real networks of support: buying groceries for a neighbor, paying someone's phone bill, offering rides to appointments, showing up for childcare. It also includes sharing knowledge and creating space for voices that often go unheard.

It means resourcing our communities with whatever we have and trusting that this flow will continue because the spirits keep us sustained. It means remembering that someone's ability to give is shaped by what they have to offer.

We do what we can, with what we have.

## The Revolution

As witches, we walk differently. We show up not only to receive, but to offer. Our magic actively redistributes both what we've inherited through systems and what we've been gifted and sustained with by the spirits.

We model what it means to live in alignment with the natural flow of give and take, rejecting anything that siphons or hoards that flow for selfish gain. This is how we change the world.

We've broken the cycle of carrying everyone else's burdens, and the spirits give us strength for the long road ahead. They offer insight for dismantling patterns of extraction, replenish us when our wells run dry, and lend us the courage and enchantment to imagine a different world.

We become bridges between the seen and the Unseen, between spirits and humans, between human communities and the land beneath our feet.

We bring radical tenderness into our communities while fiercely protecting the delicate balance of life. We rise from Her soil and reach outward, inviting others to rise with us in this shared journey of healing and restoration.

This is healing the motherline.

This is belonging to the Great Mother, weaving an ancient world anew, in freedom and with accountability.

**This is the revolution.**

# Rest Area #7

Welcome to your final Rest Area. This is a space to reflect on your current relationships and consider how you might show up in your role as a witch within your community.

**Tools You'll Need**

- A journal

- A writing utensil

1. WHAT RELATIONSHIPS IN YOUR LIFE FEEL ROOTED IN RECIPROCITY, AND WHICH ONES ASK FOR RECALIBRATION?

2. WHAT ROLE IN THE ECOSYSTEM DO YOU FEEL INSPIRED TO RECLAIM?

3. WHAT DOES RELATIONAL ACCOUNTABILITY FEEL LIKE IN YOUR BODY? IS THERE ANYWHERE YOU'RE FEELING A SENSE OF AVERSION TO RESPONSIBILITY ON A SPIRITUAL PATH?

4. WHERE HAVE YOU HISTORICALLY CONFUSED HYPER-INDEPENDENCE WITH FREEDOM? WHAT COULD INTERDEPENDENCE OFFER YOU INSTEAD?

5. WHERE, IN YOUR OWN LIFE, DO YOU SEE YOURSELF OCCUPYING POSITIONS OF SAFETY, POWER, AND PRIVILEGE WITHIN PATRIARCHY? HOW CAN YOU USE THIS TO YOUR ADVANTAGE AS A WITCH IN YOUR COMMUNITY?

6. WHAT HAS SHAPED YOUR UNDERSTANDING OF TRUST, AND HOW IS THAT SHAPING YOUR SPIRITUAL PRACTICE?

7. HOW DO YOU CARE FOR THE PLACES THAT CARE FOR YOU?

8. WHO HAS SHOWN UP FOR YOU WHEN YOU NEEDED SUPPORT? HOW DO YOU SHOW UP FOR THEM IN RETURN?

9. WHAT VERSION OF YOURSELF ARE YOU BECOMING AS YOU DEEPEN YOUR COMMITMENT TO RIGHT RELATIONSHIP?

10. WHAT ARE YOU LETTING GO TO MAKE SPACE FOR THIS NEW VERSION OF YOURSELF?

# THE NEXT THRESHOLD

We've come full circle on this path. To prepare for what lies ahead, let's ground ourselves in our ancestors' celestial worldview and reflect on what we've moved through together as an entire moon cycle.

We began in shadow. Within the quiet void of the New Moon, we set the intention to reclaim our lives as witches, living on our own terms and finding belonging beyond patriarchy.

From there, we found our footing within the animistic worldview, where light began to gather, marking our momentum into the Waxing Moon. Together, we illuminated the patriarchal wounds within the ecosystem of motorcycling and tended them with care.

As the light grew brighter, we turned inward to the motherline, honoring both the pain and the power carried in our maternal lineage. This was where our somatic practice took shape.

At the Full Moon, we saw ourselves with greater clarity. We honored all the ways our lives brought us here. We stood in our fullness and prepared to move into the Waning Moon by releasing old narratives, roles, and skins. In letting go, we made space for ongoing transformation.

We committed to bringing the gifts forged in the depths of our spirit relationships into our lives and the human world with renewed purpose, remembering that our wounds—and those of the collective—are exactly why the Great Mother called us here.

Now, we return to the New Moon. This time, we spiral forward, deepening into what we've learned and embracing our new lifelong rhythm of cycling, spiraling, and becoming.

We've moved from darkness to light and back again, each phase a turning, each turning an integration of insight. The wounds that once held us captive now open as portals. Here, you'll carry all that you've gathered and move beyond learning into action.

This next threshold gives your body time to catch up with what has been unfolding in your heart, mind, and spirit. It offers space to land, claim your practice, and affirm your commitment to riding this path with intention.

As a Biker Witch, you'll travel many roads and form all kinds of spirit relationships. Some spirits appear only once or a handful of times, while others remain with you for life, guiding, protecting, and growing alongside you.

This practice is designed to help you connect with all[1] of them, to learn from every encounter, and to engage with spirits in whatever form they arrive.

Building relationships with spirits begins by noticing the life already unfolding around you. We can easily be drawn toward distant deities, and in doing so, overlook the spirits closest to home.

Across cultures, people have long recognized the spirits who dwell in the places we live. At this threshold, we turn to those ever-present companions: House Spirits.

Your House Spirits have been with you all along. They've held space as you read this book, worked through its activities, and processed the emotional and somatic shifts that have arisen.

---

1. In *Find Your Footing*, I shared that our ancestors engaged with spirits in many different ways. The Biker Witch path follows that lineage, honoring the spirits within the Unseen dimension as I experience and interpret it, while also recognizing the indwelling spirits that inhabit the physical beings, places, and objects we can see and touch. The practice ahead engages with both, and you are welcome to approach it in whatever way feels most resonant.

Here, we pause to acknowledge them, express gratitude, and strengthen this relationship as you continue on your path. Robin Artisson, in *An Carow Gwyn: Sorcery and the Ancient Fayerie Faith*, offers a vivid glimpse into the ecology of House Spirits:

> When human beings first created permanent houses, they had to deal with the spiritual realities of the places in which they were building those dwellings. Every place in the world is already "occupied" by spirit-forces; to place a house in a location, to make a permanent change to the area, is to risk the wrath of spirits who already dwell there and who may not desire human intrusion. If spirits were amenable, it was natural that the spirits of the land who were there before would "move in" or integrate themselves with the structure of the home and its new inhabitants, becoming a new kind of social group (16).

When respected and nourished, House Spirits are known to bring good fortune, assist with housework, and offer protection[2] while you sleep and during your other spirit work.

There are two parts to this threshold ritual. First, you'll make a vow to the House Spirits in the space where you'll practice your craft, marking a shared moment of celebration as you deepen your connection with them.

If, afterwards, you feel called to create a small space in your home to make offerings, trust that call. A simple bowl of cream or a small cake left near the hearth can do wonders in thanking your House Spirits.

---

2. Opening yourself to engagement with spirits, especially those within the Unseen, is rewarding but requires awareness. Like any ecosystem, the Unseen is inhabited by a variety of beings, some of which may be predatory. In animism, spirits aren't divided by moral binaries; each has its own way of existing, which can pose risks for humans. Building relationships with protective allies, such as House Spirits, helps you navigate this complex world safely.

Second, you'll invite your motorcycle to cross this threshold *with* you. This might be the first time you recognize your motorcycle as a spirited companion, and you'll be guided in creating a special soul contract with them.

With these steps, you'll begin building reverent relationships with some of the spirits who will support you most on your journey of becoming. Your practice as a Biker Witch—as defined in this book—is now officially beginning. Let's mark it together.

## Tools You'll Need

- A bowl of whole cream

- Your motorcycle

- An offering for your motorcycle (oil change, wipe down, or a new adornment)

- A piece of paper

- A small envelope

- A writing utensil

## Make a Vow to Your House Spirits

### 1. Ground Yourself

Find a place in your home where you can connect with the spirits of the house. The ideal spot is the hearth or fireplace. If your home doesn't have a fireplace, the kitchen can serve as a symbolic hearth where warmth, nourishment, and care are both shared and received.

Stand or sit with intention in this space. Close your eyes and take a few deep breaths. Let your awareness settle into your body. Notice your heartbeat, your breath, and the presence of your home around you.

### 2. Make An Offering

Place your bowl of cream upon the hearth for the spirits of your home who have witnessed your transformations throughout this work.

You might say: "*Spirits of hearth and home,
may this offering nourish you. May my path honor you.
May I walk it well. Thank you for supporting me all this time. If it is your
will, may you continue to guide and protect me, and may my dreams and
my waking steps be touched by your wisdom as I step forward through
this next threshold.*"

### 3. Speak the Vow

When you feel ready, say these words aloud. Speak slowly, letting each line land in your body. Let your voice carry your truth.

"*I cross this next threshold to deepen into my becoming. I step onto this path with a commitment to listen and learn. I return to the web of life and I vow to walk in right relationship with you and all other beings, seen and Unseen.*"

You can repeat this as many times as you need. You can change the words if something truer rises in you.

## 4. Listen

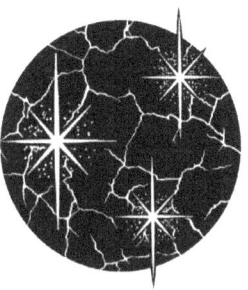

Sit for a few moments in quiet with your home, witnessing with presence as the House Spirits have done for you.

## 5. Close with Touch

Place your hand on your heart, your belly, or the hearth. Anchor the ritual with your touch. Whisper a thank you. When you're ready, move to Part 2.

# Invite Your Motorcycle

### 1. Arrive in Sacred Space

Stand or sit with your motorcycle. Let yourself arrive fully.

You might say: *"I greet you as a companion. I recognize your spirit. I honor your strength. You have carried me, and I ask that you carry me still. I invite you to cross this next threshold* with me, to deepen our relationship into one of trust, care, and shared becoming."

### 2. Make an Offering

This can be as simple or ceremonial as you'd like. Offer your care, a symbolic object, or a gesture of love to your bike.

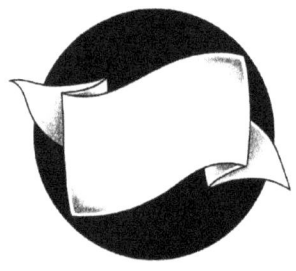

### 3. Write Your Contract

Write a promise to your motorcycle in a way that upholds reciprocity. You can use the words below or modify them to suit your truth:

*"This is a vow between soul and steel. I commit to listening when you speak, whether in sound, sensation, or silence. I will care for you as I care for myself. I will not ask you to carry what I am not willing to hold with you. In return, I ask that you hold me safely. Together, we will cross thresholds, ride the currents of the Unseen, and weave magic into the world. We are in this together through the wind, the quiet, the unknown, and the return."*

### 4. Anchor the Bond

Anchor your bond by placing your contract
in a small envelope and carrying it
somewhere on your bike. You might tuck
it in your saddlebag, slip it into your tool
roll, or hide it in your gear.

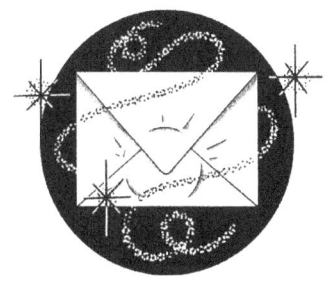

Say: "Let this hold our bond. Let this carry our vow. Let this
remind us we ride together."

### 5. Close with Touch

Place one hand on your heart and one hand
on your bike. Anchor the ritual with your
touch. Whisper a thank you. Then slowly
return to the rest of your day.

You've crossed the threshold and made your vow. You've honored both
your body and your bike.

You've declared your presence as someone who listens, who honors,
and who walks in right relationship.

Welcome. You're ready.

# THE ROUTE

# Witchcraft in Motion

The route I've carved out for you here is designed to support your becoming without ever limiting what you choose to let shape you along the way. It holds both structure and spaciousness, left intentionally simple so you can develop your own practice within it.

At its core, the path of the Biker Witch is centered on cultivating reverent relationships with spirits. We do this by inviting them to meet us where we are, just as we learn to meet them where they are. Our ancestors are often the first spirits willing to bridge that distance, guiding us into the wider web of relationship.

As Sadee Whip states in *Savage Awakening: Initiatory Paths of the Dragon Mother:*

> Our ancestors are some of the only spirit beings who have what we call a vested interest in our well-being. We have blood ties to them. We have history and imprints from many of them. For some of us, our bodies were made from the same land as their bodies were made (225).

Your ancestors stand ready to support you as you take your place in the lineage of healing and magic. They know who you are, recognize what you carry, and understand the importance of the work you're doing.

Rooting into relationship with your ancestors also helps you sift through what your conditioned mind might question or doubt.

We know our ancestors are real because we exist as a result of them. Their presence is a truth woven into our bodies and lives, grounding our journey of transformation in lineage, where the work remains both personal and intimate.

Another reason to begin with your ancestors is accessibility. It doesn't matter where your ancestors come from, whether you know their origins, or if you have close ties to your family. You don't need perfect connections to your relatives, living or deceased, to start this work.

Each of us can call on our Well Ancestors.[1] Having lived and died so long ago, they have had time to rest, to heal, and to return to the arms of the Great Mother. They are safe to turn toward and will offer profound insight.

Beyond the altar, as we explored in *Rubber Meets The Road*, the spirits of place[2] share more about themselves with us as we move through their realms. In many animist traditions, these spirits are understood as ancient beings who existed long before humans.

They are elders of the land, often considered ancestors in their own right. They remember how the world came to be and carry a knowing from long before memory. When we approach them with reverence and offerings, many are willing to share their wisdom and gifts with us.

Alongside your motorcycle and your House Spirits, the ancestors and the spirits of place will participate in your becoming, informing the power you are learning to carry. They respond

---

1. Those who lived in the world before patriarchy. While their lives were not free of hardship, their challenges arose from natural cycles and ancestral trials, burdens carried within the rhythms of survival and renewal. This stands in contrast to the compounded trauma imposed by colonial systems, which fractured those rhythms and transformed struggle into systemic oppression.

2. Sprits of place: The conscious, sentient presence inherent in a particular landscape. These spirits may exist as a singular dominant entity, a collective of multiple entities, or a shifting network of presences, and they vary from place to place. Many landscapes also carry the spirits of deceased humans and non-human beings, whose continued presence contributes to the vitality, memory, and relational dynamics of the land. Recognizing spirits of place emphasizes that every location is alive, responsive, and unique in its expression of life.

to how you show up, how you ride, and how you listen. These relationships invite you into the past and the present, into stillness and movement, and into what is both seen and unseen.

**This is witchcraft in motion.**

It reminds us that magic isn't fixed or theoretical. It's alive. It breathes. It moves. The ritual arc I offer here opens with intention and presence, deepens through engagement, and closes in gratitude and integration. It creates a strong container for your transformations while honoring the ever-shifting dance between you and the spirits.

.⁺✦

## Timing

You'll time your practice by aligning it with the cycles of the moon. The moon is a constant companion. She changes with us, and each of her phases offers a new way to move through your becoming and build on the transformations that have already occurred.

Her rhythm not only marks time but also shapes intention. It helps you tune into what you're truly asking the spirits for, what's ready to be seen, what needs to be shed, and what's asking to be honored within you as part of your ever-evolving nature.

The moon is one of the first beings our ancestors learned to count on. Her glow lit the night sky, her tides shaped the land. She guided planting, harvesting, dreaming, and divining. Her presence continues in your life, marking time as steady movement and reminding you there's no need to rush or force transformation.

You too are meant to move in phases. There will be times when you can't get on your bike because the weather shifted, your motorcycle needs repairs, or your body or spirit isn't ready. Even then, the moon will rise. She offers a place to return to, no matter where you are. When you can't ride, you can still observe, still listen, and still offer.

We time our practice with the moon because her cycles of waxing, fullness, waning, and rest teach us how to grow, how to let go, how to soften, and how to begin again. She is a celestial guide and a daughter of the Great Mother, in harmony with the cycles of birth, death, and renewal that pulse through the Earth and all beings.

When you follow the moon, you walk in step with the Great Mother herself. You move with a rhythm older than any calendar. As you begin to pay closer attention, you may find your own emotional or energetic rhythms echoing hers. This too is part of the journey. You're learning to move with what is.

## Opening

The altar is where every ritual begins. It's a special space shared between you and the spirits. Here, you open through presence. You show up with your questions, your grief, your offerings, and your gratitude. The altar is where relationships are built and where ritual gains depth and direction.

Because your ancestors are some of your most consistent guides in this work, your altar becomes a meeting place for dialogue with them. It's as much a space for speaking from the heart as it is for quieting the mind and listening.

Opening your practice at the altar allows you to draw strength and wisdom from the past. You are not doing this work in isolation. You are not the beginning of the story.

You are part of a long lineage, and your place within it matters. When you sit at the altar, you acknowledge this truth. You say yes to being in relationship with what came before and what continues to develop.

## Deepening

After opening at the altar, leaving your offerings, and asking your ancestors to support your becoming, you take to the open road to deepen your engagement with other beings.

Riding opens us in ways few other practices can. On a motorcycle, we are fully immersed. The land becomes something we feel not just beneath us, but all around us. Through this embodied presence, we come into contact with the spirits of place.

Every place carries its own spirits, and many landscapes have their own collective voice. Some spirits may welcome you warmly, while others may be cautious. Some may require more than one visit to engage with you. Some may ask you to leave, and others might request something in return. The only way to know is to listen.

With every new area we enter, we become guests. The practice of riding with reverence begins with remembering this. These lands are not ours to take or conquer, they are beings to be greeted and honored.

One way to show respect is by riding with awareness and gratitude. This means acknowledging the spirits of each place as you pass through. A simple word of thanks as you cross a mountain pass or descend into a valley can carry weight.

Every devotional ritual ride includes taking the time to stop and connect with the spirits of place. You'll pull off the road, walk a short distance into the trees, and sit in stillness. The practice of quietly sitting with the land is found in many cultures.

In Norse tradition, it's called útiseta: sitting out on the land to listen, receive vision, and commune with spirits. While útiseta may not come from your direct lineage, its wisdom is universal. Sitting with the land in this way invites humility and relationship.

When you can't ride, you can still meet the spirits of place. Walk a familiar trail or sit beneath a nearby tree. The spirits aren't limited to remote forests or scenic overlooks. They are wherever you are willing to meet them.

Building relationships with the spirits of place requires trust. It means showing up as a guest and leaving as a friend. These spirits feel your care and your intention. In time, they will share their magic to support your becoming.

## Returning

Your return from the ride is just as important as your departure. This is the time to reflect, to gently trace the contours of what unfolded. Return to your altar and speak to your ancestors. Tell them what you discovered. If the wind gave you peace, let them feel it through your breath.

If a hawk circled overhead and brought you to tears, let that moment land in their presence. If a stranger's kindness opened something new inside you, offer that too. This is how relationship deepens.

After you speak, give the story a place to live outside your mind. Let it take shape in your journal. Record the ritual from start to finish: what surfaced at the altar before you left, what rose during the ride, what felt sacred, what felt strange, the moments that made you laugh, and the moments that left you speechless.

## Closing

Before closing the ritual, ask your ancestors for a dream that continues the conversation, one that offers clarity or reveals a shift in direction. Carrying them into other parts of your life tells them you are listening.

It opens the door for insight to rise through the dark waters of the night. Keep your journal by your bed and be prepared to record your dreams as soon as you wake in the morning.

## Listening

Sometimes the work we do with spirits takes time to appear in our lives. Whether we're sitting quietly at the altar or riding through spirited landscapes, we're always engaging in conversation. The change begins there and often emerges later, sometimes in ways we don't expect.

Listening for change is a skill we learn slowly. Spirits speak in many languages. You might feel a shift in your body, a sudden knowing you can't explain, or the lifting of an emotional weight. Their messages might come through uncanny moments and coincidences.

You may hear a song at the perfect time or receive an unexpected note from someone you haven't spoken to in years. At my college graduation party, for instance, a Lynyrd Skynyrd song suddenly blasted at full volume. We all laughed, knowing it was my mom turning up the party.

Dreams remain one of the oldest ways of conversing with spirits, which is why I've woven the practice of asking for a dream into these rituals. I've dreamt of my mother three times since beginning this work. In each dream, we sit at a picnic table surrounded by greenery and sunlight.

She is always vibrant, the age she was when she passed, telling me she's okay. The dream isn't about her death but her aliveness and where she is now. It doesn't feel like a puzzle to decode but a visit, a truth that she's at peace.

There were also stretches when I stopped showing up at the altar, and during those times my friends dreamed of my mom. She came to them with messages and gifts instead. Once she told Sadee to give me a puppy, which was both mind-blowing and perfect.

When I was seven, my mom had gifted me a puppy, so she knew I'd understand when Sadee passed on the dream. None of my friends had ever met her, and it still makes me giggle how persistent she is, even in spirit.

Spirits might also speak through the land itself. As you ride, you might feel your chest soften and your mind clear. Passing through certain places, you may feel watched. Sometimes it's a gentle observation, other times a firm warning to leave. The more we listen, the more fluent we become in their language.

One of the most important lessons I've learned is to let spirits be as they are. We don't need to force their presence into meaning through our human lenses.

An owl on the road doesn't have to signify death or insight; it can simply be an owl. Notice how it moves, how it looks at you. Stay present with its being and ask what it might be teaching you instead of assuming.

The same is true of a mother deer and her speckled fawn by the roadside. They don't need to symbolize divine femininity or personal healing. They are simply mother and child, embodying the living intelligence of care, protection, and instinct. That alone is meaningful.

We learn from their wisdom by witnessing them and allowing their presence to matter as it is, not by interpreting, decoding, or turning them into symbols of the human condition. Spirit work is a slow practice of listening with curiosity until something deeper begins to speak.

Give it time. Transformation will come like rain after a long dry spell. It will gather slowly, soak in, and feel real in your body. Spirits don't rush. Ancestors don't push. Keep riding. Keep showing up with sincerity and openness. The rest will reveal itself when the time is right.

## Carrying

As you move through your practice, consider which parts of your transformation are meant to flow back into the web of life. Some wisdom is not only for you; it is meant to be shared.

It may appear as a story that opens another's heart, an offering of time, skill, or care to beings human or otherwise, or simply a new way of moving through the world that others can feel in your presence. Be ready to carry what you learn forward, weaving it into your days and into the communities to which you belong.

## Evolving

Let this be a path you explore, expand, and weave with your own traditions and ceremonies. You are wholeheartedly invited to take detours, make unexpected stops, and follow your own side quests as they arise.

These aren't distractions but part of the magic itself, and they are often exactly what the spirits want to share with you. Trust what feels most alive and true in each moment.

# THE TOOLS

# Gather Your Tools

As a Biker Witch, the tools you work with will become some of your closest allies. They support your spells, hold space for your inner transformations, and offer tangible ways to stay in communication with spirits in your daily life.

It's time to gather your tools for this specific route. The list I share here comes directly from my own practice. You are welcome to expand beyond what is offered, but I recommend starting with these.

You likely already have some of these items, and if they still feel aligned with the spirit communication you will be embracing on this path, keep them in your tool box.

If there are items you don't yet have, or if you feel called to find new allies for this journey, consider this an invitation to embark on a special adventure to find them. Finding the right allies to support you is part of the magic, and it's also part of the fun.

This process of gathering your tools is a signal to the spirits and to your own soul that you are preparing yourself for powerful connection. You're not just collecting things; you are gathering allies for healing, protection, creation, and deeper vision. Make it as ceremonial and special as you and these beings deserve.

## Tools List

- Ancestor Altar Surface

- Offerings dish(es)

- Candle(s)

- A candle snuffer

- Spirit journal

- Container(s) for Roadside Offerings

- Moon Timing Tool

- Divination tool(s)

- Optional: photos of ancestors, incense, small items that feel meaningful or supportive, and books or stories connected to your lineage or ancestral themes

## Ancestor Altar

There are many ways to create an altar, and there is no single "right" way to begin. Some witches build multiple altars throughout their homes for ancestors, deities, household spirits, and land spirits. As a Biker Witch, you'll be creating an ancestor altar. Even if you create others later, I suggest keeping your ancestor altar active and tended with regular offerings.

What you place on your ancestor altar is entirely up to you. Altars evolve as we do. They grow, shift, and reflect where we are in our lives and practices. My altar includes a few constants year-round, along with items that change with the seasons or during ancestral holy days. I'll share how I developed my own ancestor altar and how I maintain and engage with it.

Feel free to take whatever resonates with you from my practice and shape it into something that feels right for your path. Sometimes, our ancestors will guide us in how these spaces should look and feel, so listen closely for their input.

Most importantly, care for your altar as you would your home for a beloved guest. Keep it clean, tended, and alive. This is where your relationship with the ancestors begins to take shape, and keeping it fresh is part of how we honor them.

**Surface:** My altar is an old sewing table I found at a local antique store. It was dusty and forgotten, but I felt drawn to it. I loved its shape, the height, and the way its two tiers seemed made to hold candles on one level and offerings on the other. When we moved to New Orleans, it was one of the few items I insisted on bringing. That kind of attachment is what I believe every witch deserves to feel for their altar. I painted it purple simply because it needed to be. I never questioned it.

When searching for your own perfect altar, you might be surprised by what draws your eye. It could be an old dresser, a nightstand, or a full table. Let yourself touch it, sit near it, talk to it, and notice what arises in that exchange. You might already have something at home, like the corner of a dresser, your grandmother's old foot bench you remember sitting on as a kid, or a shelf you've kept in the garage for years and never quite managed to let go of.

Once you've found the surface you want to use, choose a spot in your home where you can be undisturbed during rituals. This space becomes your landing pad, used before and after rides, so try to make it both accessible and protected—a place where offerings can remain without being moved. You might want to close a door or create a boundary to keep pets or others out.

**Offering Dishes:** I have three small offering dishes—one for liquids, one for solids, and one fire-safe bowl for incense. Sometimes I use all three, and other times just one. My dishes were a gift from Sadee, and they bring me so much joy to look at and work with. Find a dish, or dishes, that feel like what it would be like to break out the "good china" for a special occasion, even if that "good china" is chipped, well-loved, speckled with snake-skin patterns, or doused in glitter.

**Candles:** I always keep at least one candle on my altar. Candles help me mark the opening and closing of the rituals that take place there.

**Candle Snuffer:** I use a candle snuffer to put out the flames after my rituals because I prefer to extinguish the flame gently rather than blowing it out.

**Photos:** Many animist traditions suggest placing only photos of Well Ancestors on the altar. Personally, I include my more recently departed, even if they are still becoming Well.[1] Seeing my mother's face while I place a cigarette on the altar for her, or my nana's smile as I pour her coffee, deepens my connection to them. These acts feel like rituals of love and remembrance and are part of healing the ancestral line. With discernment, you can

---

1. When an ancestor is becoming Well, it means they are moving toward restoration and healing beyond death, finding wholeness that may have been disrupted in life. Our work to decolonize our minds, bodies, and communities contributes to this process, repairing fractures imposed by colonial systems and transforming the legacy they left behind.

include ancestors who are still in the process of healing, while calling on the Well ones to support you. **One teaching shared across many traditions is to avoid placing items or photos of anyone who is still alive on your ancestor altar.**

**Around the altar:** I keep items that help me feel close to my ancestors, such as folkloric books from my ancestral regions, my mother's perfume, incense crafted specifically for ancestor reverence, and small objects from nature that ground me when I am in a meditative state.

## Spirit Journal

You may already be using a journal to track your journey, especially during the Rest Areas in this book. I invite you to choose another one specifically for your practice. This spirit journal becomes a vessel for the story of your becoming, capturing the ways your life evolves through rituals and conversations. Over time, it grows into a witness, reflecting the transformations within you and the evolving relationship you are building with spirit beings, and with yourself.

My own journal appeared when I wasn't even searching. It's a brown leather notebook embossed with a tree. The moment I saw it, I knew it was the one. The tree felt like the perfect symbol for ancestor reverence. It has become the place where I record my becoming, knowing that the changes within me ripple outward, transforming my family tree.

You will use this journal to record your rituals, as well as the messages, dreams, and moments you receive from spirits. Let it move with you between the altar and your bedside, ready to hold your dreams in the morning. You may also wish to divide it into sections, with the first half dedicated to altar practice and the second half reserved for synchronicities, dreams, and spirit communications.

## Containers for Roadside Offerings

Choose a sealable container that can travel with you. It should be sturdy enough to hold liquid or solid biodegradable offerings for the spirits of place. You might also bring a second container, like a shot glass or small bowl, to hold your offerings while you sit with the spirits. Pouring into this dish before returning the offering to the earth honors the spirits with a toast before the gift returns to the land.

These containers are more than practical. They carry both our offerings and our intentions. They remind us that reverence and reciprocity are not one-time acts, but ongoing commitments to live in a way that holds us accountable to the web of life.

Many of the lands you'll travel through carry the trauma of colonization. Each time you fill a container, take a moment to learn the history of the land you're on and the lands along your route. A brief search can uncover the names of the Indigenous peoples who have long belonged to these places. It can also offer insight into the kinds of offerings that are most respectful to the spirits, and that contribute to healing and repair.

The ceremonious act of filling your container can be paired with planning a route that includes intentional stops to support Indigenous-owned businesses and restaurants, or to engage with local Indigenous communities in other ways when welcomed. Local museums, parks, and historical societies can also deepen your understanding of what was stolen and what must be returned.

Further, I recommend making it a consistent practice to contribute financially to Indigenous-led mutual aid campaigns or to volunteer your time in support of Land Back efforts. Think of it like paying a toll on a freeway or paying rent for practicing your spirituality on stolen land. It's an acknowledgment of the cost these lands and the Indigenous peoples who belong to them have carried.

These moments are how we honor Indigenous sovereignty and take responsibility for repair by going beyond sitting out from systems that harm. They open the possibility of finding your place within a deeper story of justice and restitution.

## Moon Timing Tool

You'll need something to help you track lunar time. This doesn't have to be elaborate. It can be a printed lunar calendar, a handmade chart kept near your altar, or even an app that helps you stay attuned to the changing phases. What matters is that it becomes something you return to regularly, a way to stay connected to the rhythm that supports your practice.

## Divination Tool(s)

In a devotional, offerings-based practice, divination becomes a way of entering into dialogue with the Unseen. Allies such as tarot cards, runes, or oracle decks can help you tune into the guidance of spirits, your own intuition, and the movements of your transformation.

You don't need to be an expert to begin. Choose a method that feels familiar or resonates, perhaps one your ancestors once used, and allow your relationship with it to develop over time. If tarot feels overwhelming, begin with a single card. If you feel drawn to runes or bones, trust that pull and see where it leads.

Keep your chosen tool near your altar so it becomes part of your daily rhythm. Between ritual rides, it can serve as a daily invitation to place an offering on your altar and open conversation with your ancestors or other spirit guides.

Alright, Biker Witch. Now you have a sense of what witchcraft in motion really looks like, and you've gathered your tools. Go ahead and add them to your toolbox and grab your keys. It's time to go your own way.

# GRAB YOUR KEYS

# Go Your Own Way

As I wave you off to go your own way, I'm offering two levels of engagement for your practice. You can choose whichever aligns with your current capacity and the natural rhythms in which that capacity fluctuates. These levels aren't meant to measure skill, but to help you reflect on how often you can engage in intentional spirit communion in a way that feels sustainable.

As you grow more attuned to your energy and needs, you can move fluidly between the levels, scaling back when life feels full or deepening your practice when the call arises. There are no rigid rules for how to engage with this path. Think of it as an ongoing conversation with life rather than a fixed system.

Before we explore the two levels, I'll share foundational considerations for working with spirits. From there, you can sense which rhythm feels most accessible to you right now. I'll also offer[1] guidance on setting intentions for each moon cycle, crafting calls to ancestors and the spirits of place, selecting offerings, and documenting your experiences in your spirit journal.

Depending on your capacity in any given month, your rhythm might include one or two devotional ritual rides. These rides create space to offer, listen, and commune with your ancestors and the spirits of place. They invite presence, reverence, and the

---

1. What I've created here is inspired by and adapted from Sadee Whip's approach to altar work, as shared in her book *Savage Awakening: Initiatory Paths of the Dragon Mother*. I highly recommend reading it. Sadee provides clear guidance and language that can support both your altar practice and your relationships with spirits.

opportunity to carry forward the wisdom you receive, sustaining your life and shaping your becoming as a Biker Witch.

As your practice expands, you may feel drawn to honor specific deities, explore ancestral traditions, or deepen your connection with other beings. Everything in this book is meant to give you a strong foundation, providing the language and lenses to support all areas of your workings as a witch.

What you cultivate through this devotional, offerings-based practice carries over into your other magical work. The living intelligence the spirits share with you becomes a guide, strengthening your power, refining your intuition, and rooting your practice ever more deeply in the Great Mother.

During the other phases of the moon cycle, you're invited to engage in intentional spell work and rituals in response to what you receive from your spirit allies during and after your rides. Working with each lunar phase helps you draw on its energy and keeps you in a consistent rhythm of practicing your craft, even when you're not on the road.

While I don't provide step-by-step instructions for specific spells and rituals tied to these phases, many trusted resources are available elsewhere. Concepts from earlier chapters can help you approach them with discernment, adapting them to reflect your personal path and uphold right relationship. Let this be a time to get creative and enjoy exploring different workings.

Finally, I will close out our time together by providing visual examples of a complete month for both levels.

## Foundations for Spirit Communion

**Don't make promises to spirits that you can't keep.** If you speak at your altar and say you'll return tomorrow, then you must return tomorrow. If you tell the spirits of a place that you will bring an offering next week but later choose to take a different route, understand that you are working with beings who remember and who are in relationship with you. Trust is built through your follow-through and consistency. Showing up when you say you will is one of the simplest and most powerful ways to build integrity in these relationships.

**Consent is just as important in the spirit world as it is in human relationships.** Spirits are not here to serve you, nor do they owe you anything. If you approach a hill and ask to introduce yourself to the land but receive a feeling or message that you should leave, honor that. If you reach for an herb to include in a remedy and they say no, respect that boundary. Never assume access simply because you are curious or well-intentioned.

**Come as you are, but come with respect.** Take responsibility for how you're showing up. If you are angry, agitated, or in a state that makes it difficult to connect, it may be best to wait and return another day. Like any relationship, this work asks for honesty about your capacity in the moment. Some days you will show up raw and emotional. Other days you may need to postpone. Both are important, and learning to recognize your readiness is part of the practice.

**Spirits can surprise you.** You might be trying to connect with your grandmother and instead hear from a distant uncle you never knew, or a guide may appear with a request you didn't expect. Offerings might shift based on what the spirits actually ask for, not what you planned. Sometimes a message will come that isn't even for you, but for someone else. Stay open to what emerges.

**Spirit communication is not a transaction.** Avoid approaching it with the mindset of "I do this so I get that." Come not only when you want something, but also to express gratitude, to witness, or simply to be present.

**Offerings are not payments.** They are gestures of relationship. Ask what is welcome and be ready to listen. In some cases, no offering is needed beyond your attention and respect. In others, something very specific may be asked of you. What matters is that the offering reflects the sincerity of your relationship, not a sense of obligation.

**Land has memory.** Before entering into a relationship with the spirits of place, take time to acknowledge the history of the land itself. What has this place endured? Colonization, extraction, violence, and displacement leave imprints that don't disappear. Listening includes acknowledging the grief as much as beauty. You are stepping into a story that began long before you arrived. Let your reverence include that awareness.

## Finding Your Moon Rhythm

This practice is anchored in the lunar cycle because it encourages regular engagement without pressure. Alongside these moon rhythms, I encourage you to honor your ancestral and personal holy days. These may be rooted in celebration, remembrance, or quiet reflection, and they can take place at your altar, in nature, or within the stillness of your own home.

You might choose to weave these sacred days into your devotional riding practice or allow them to stand on their own. They become especially powerful during times when riding isn't possible, such as in winter or periods of rest. These days offer continuity, keeping your practice alive and your spirit companions close.

Both levels of this work are crafted with the assumption that you will maintain a consistent offerings practice at your altar for your ancestors throughout the month, ideally daily. Even when you're not riding or engaging in a full ritual, you remain in relationship. A brief daily visit to leave an offering, ask a question, pull a card, or speak a simple word of gratitude is enough to keep them sustained as they continue providing for you until your next intentional engagement.

I recommend using the days leading into each New Moon as a time to check in and assess your rhythm for the cycle ahead. The New Moon offers a natural invitation to reflect on what you have the capacity for in the coming weeks, both in your life and in your work with spirits.

This can be a helpful time to map out your month, marking the moon cycle dates and planning when you can complete rituals or move through spells. You might also notice an upcoming holy day you want to weave into a ritual or honor in its own way. Taking this time for reflection helps you move forward with clarity and can build a sense of anticipation and excitement around your practice.

If you plan to do at least one ride for the moon cycle ahead, I recommend making sure it's the New Moon ride. After the ride, your month can unfold in a way that suits your chosen rhythm, whether that includes additional rituals or spell work during other moon phases, a second ritualized ride, or simply allowing your becoming to bloom while continuing with regular altar tending and devotional acts until the next New Moon.

It's worth noting that your ritual rides don't need to happen entirely at night. You might choose to ride at dusk, when there is still daylight but the moon is visible, timing your return to the altar after dark. This allows you to embrace the beauty of both day and evening, while letting the night deepen your connection. Though I will say, sitting out with the land spirits at night can be an especially potent experience.

## Biker Witch Engagement Levels

The ritual rides I've created take place either on the New Moon alone or on both the New and Full Moon. Fixed points like these make planning easier, while the waxing and waning phases provide more flexible windows for ongoing practice. By balancing structure and flexibility, you gain the freedom to shape the practice in a way that works for you.

## Light Engagement: New Moon Ride

Includes one full ritual ride each moon cycle, centered on the New Moon. Throughout the month, you continue tending your altar and leaving offerings. This rhythm supports connection during busy seasons, periods of rest, or times when your energy feels low, while still honoring the relationships that hold and guide you.

Even a lighter practice is meaningful when your attention is sincere and your intention is clear. You might also weave in spell work and rituals during the month that respond to what has been emerging since your New Moon ride.

**Waxing Moon:** Focus on what is beginning to take root in your becoming. Consider a working that deepens your relationship with what is emerging. Pay attention to what feels tender, exciting, or uncertain.

**Full Moon:** Return to your altar and share with your ancestors what has become clear. Celebrate your progress and notice what the full light reveals that no longer feels supportive. Sit with these truths, allowing yourself to grow ready to release them in the Waning Moon phase ahead.

**Waning Moon:** Turn inward and reflect on what you are being called to take responsibility for, as well as what you're being called to release. Use this phase to let go of what no longer serves your path, clearing space for what is yet to come.

## Balanced Engagement: New Moon and Full Moon

Includes ritualized rides on the New Moon and the Full Moon. You might set an intention at the New Moon and, at the Full Moon, revisit your progress, honor your growth, and notice what no longer serves your becoming under the full illumination.

This rhythm invites growth, clarity, and deeper dialogue with spirits. Between ritual rides, your ongoing altar tending continues to nurture your relationships and keep the channel of communication open. You might also weave in spell work and rituals during the month as mid-way points that respond to what has been emerging since your New and Full Moon rides.

**Waxing Moon:** Focus on what is beginning to take root in your becoming. Consider a working that deepens your relationship with what is emerging. Pay attention to what feels tender, exciting, or uncertain.

**Waning Moon:** Turn inward and reflect on what you are being called to take responsibility for, as well as what you're being called to release. Use this phase to let go of what no longer serves your path, clearing space for what is yet to come.

## Planting Seeds of Intention

Setting intentions for your becoming can feel daunting, especially when you're not entirely sure what you're seeking or what the spirits want or need from you. One way to begin is by reflecting on the themes woven throughout this book and noticing how they show up in your own life.

Your intentions might center on how to return to the Great Mother through small, tangible steps. This could look like leaving behind life within patriarchy, tending to your healing needs, navigating relationships, exploring your ancestral inheritance, walking your path as a witch, weathering the storms of your initiatory journey, or discerning what to hold and what to release as part of your own dynamic becoming.

The season you find yourself in, both outer and inner, can also shape what you ask for or how you listen. Spring may call you to consider what is ready to bloom, where new beginnings want to take hold. Autumn's cooler air might invite reflection on what can be let go, what is ready to die as a natural part of life. Paying attention to these rhythms can deepen your relationship with the cycles around you, including the ones within.

Intentions don't need to be grand or poetic. You might be beginning the slow process of leaving a toxic relationship, knowing it will take time and courage, and ask your spirit allies for strength and guidance. You might want to learn a new skill that brings you closer to your calling and ask the spirits what the first step might be.

If you're a parent, your intention might be to find moments of presence and softness amid chaos. You might simply ask to be shown what you are ready to see as a way of reconnecting to that presence and softness.

When in doubt, or if you feel unmoored in the unknown, ask yourself what you need right now to become more of who you already are. What would help you live more in alignment with your values? What kind of support would feel steady enough to hold you as you grow? What boundaries might help support your intention?

If you don't know, that's okay. This is where a divination tool can be a powerful ally. Pull a card to ask your spirit guides what is ready to be healed, seen, or tended. Sometimes we don't yet have the words for what we already know to be true. Divination can help bring shape to what is still forming and open the way toward clearer conversation with it.

## Crafting a Call

Crafting a call to spirits is a way of intentionally reaching out and inviting the presence or guidance of spirits into the moment with you. Often, a call is just a few words that you'll find yourself repeating at the start of every ritual. Since you'll be working with both your ancestors at your altar and the spirits of place in different locations, you will likely create two separate calls.

For your ancestors, choose two words that feel meaningful to you and your lineage, capturing aspects of their wisdom, power, magic, or guidance.

**Here are a few prompts to help you find your words:**

Think of qualities or gifts your ancestors are known for in your family or lineage. What two words capture those?

Consider what you most want to honor or call upon in this moment. Which two words express that?

**Example formats:**

- Ancestors of Wisdom and Strength

- Ancestors of Courage and Guidance

- Ancestors of Magic and Resilience

- Ancestors of Healing and Vision

For the spirits of place, you can use phrasing that is adaptable to the many landscapes you'll engage with, honoring both the space and the spirits present.

A simple and effective example is: "Spirits of (location)." You can be more specific if the moment calls for it, adjusting your words to the energy and context of each location.

## Offerings

**Ancestor Offerings:** When making offerings, consider what would feel culturally relevant and meaningful to your ancestors. This might involve researching foods or drinks they cherished, a song to sing or poem to recite, flowers they loved, or lighting incense with a scent familiar or significant to them.

Many ancestral practices were disrupted or erased by colonization and never formally recorded, so much of what remains has been preserved through folklore, stories, and mythology passed down orally. Treat these stories as a map, guiding you in shaping offerings that honor their legacy.

Offerings thought to hold a lot of life force, such as cream, butter, whiskey, or ale, are considered especially nourishing for spirits. This is not a literal measure of energy, but a recognition that these items are rich and full of vitality. Their significance comes from both their inherent qualities and the intention behind the offering, making them a meaningful gesture of care and connection.

My own offerings vary depending on the day. Sometimes it's a simple cup of cream; other times, a beer or a sweet treat I've made in the kitchen. These small gestures keep my ancestors woven into my daily life as an intentional act of nourishment for both them and me, even on busy days.

On occasions like Samhain, when the energy feels more festive and I have more time and space, I prepare more elaborate offerings that often require a special shopping trip to acquire items my more recently deceased ancestors would love. I might buy my mother's favorite cigarettes and a Snickers bar, my grandfather's favorite candy and beer, and prepare a cherished ancestral recipe.

Think of ancestor offerings as cooking for the family you love. Sometimes it's a full and generous spread, other times a small treat or a shared cup of coffee. Either way, the care and intention remain the same.

**Offerings for the Spirits of Place:** Offerings for spirits of place can vary depending on the location. Some spirits simply want your presence and attention, others appreciate a gesture of kindness or an act of service, and some may welcome a physical offering.

The safest approach is to always carry a physical offering in your roadside container. From there, remain attentive and open, letting the spirits of place guide you in the moment.

When giving a physical offering, keep it simple, respectful, and biodegradable. Choose items that won't disrupt the local ecosystem, such as a splash of cream, a small bit of organic honey, or water infused with love and gratitude. You can place your offering container directly on the earth, or, if you find a flat surface like a stone or a log, you can create a temporary roadside altar.

A gesture of kindness or act of service can look like picking up litter or gently moving an animal kin that has passed near the road so they may return to the earth.

As you continue building your relationships with the spirits of place, especially at locations you return to repeatedly, you will develop a deeper sense of what they appreciate and how they wish to be honored.

**Discarding Offerings:** When it's time to discard offerings, do so with gratitude. Consider the energy of the offering as "spent" because the spirits have consumed and enjoyed it. Return it to the earth or place it in the compost pile, honoring the exchange that has taken place.

## Writing It Down

Your journal serves two intertwined purposes: to document the ritual itself and to track the magic that continues afterward. Begin by recording the details of your ritualized ride, noting the moon phase, your intention for the cycle, the date, and the time.

Describe the ride from start to finish: how you opened the ritual, what offerings were made, the questions you asked, what you shared with your ancestors or the spirits of place, what occurred during the ride, and what transpired upon your return. This creates a step-by-step picture of the experience, giving your ritual form and clarity in writing.

In addition to documenting the ride itself, use your journal to track the magic that arises over time. Note moments of strangeness, epiphanies, dreams, intuitive insights, or any moments of knowing that connect back to your practice. Include the date and time for each entry, and capture everything you wish to remember.

You can also record your other moon phase rituals if you choose. How you tell the story of your becoming is entirely up to you. Over time, your spirit journal becomes a personal archive of how spirits have been a part of your days, and a place to return for inspiration whenever you need to find your way back to this path.

# A Biker Witch's Devotional Practice: Visual Flow

Light Engagement: *New Moon Ride*

| Before the Ride |
|:---:|
| ☾ Light a candle to open your ritual. |
| ☾ Call to your ancestors. |
| ☾ Place your offering for them upon your altar. |
| ☾ Tell your ancestors what day and time it is. Share a bit about your day, as if you were speaking with a long-distance friend. |
| ☾ Share your intention for the month ahead. Speak from your heart and ask for the support you need, in whatever form it may come. |
| ☾ Thank your ancestors for their guidance, their love, and their protection. |
| ☾ Leave your offering on the altar for your ancestors to enjoy in your absence, and let them know you will return after your ride. |
| ☾ Gently snuff out your candle, holding the intention of re-lighting it upon your return. |

## During the Ride

☾ Go for your ride and find a place to sit out.

☾ Ask the land for permission to be there and feel into whether you're welcome.

☾ If you are welcome, settle in. If not, keep riding until you find your yes.

☾ After receiving a yes, let your breath and body become part of the space.

☾ Call to the spirits of place. Speak or feel your invitation for connection.

☾ Offer your gratitude in whatever way is asked. You might place a physical offering from your container upon the earth, take a sacred action, or simply be present.

☾ Introduce yourself. Tell the spirits who you are, why you've come, and how grateful you are to share this time.

☾ Listen. Witness.

☾ When you're ready to hit the road again, give thanks. Acknowledge the spirits' presence and the time you've shared.

☾ Close with care. Return your physical offering to the earth, or if your gift is your presence, leave a loving touch on the land as you part.

## The Return

☾ Return to your altar.

☾ Re-light your candle.

☾ Call to your ancestors once more.

☾ Share with your ancestors what you experienced during your ride, offering your reflections as a closing gift.

☾ Thank your ancestors for listening to you and witnessing you today.

☾ Ask them for a dream and tell them when you will return to your altar to connect with them again.

☾ When you're ready, snuff out your candle to close the ritual.

☾ Write in your journal. Record your experiences and any initial impressions or guidance that came through.

☾ Jot down the whole ritual from beginning to end.

☾ Respectfully discard your offerings and take your journal with you to bed.

**Optional:**

Waxing Moon: A Ritual for Deepening

Full Moon: A Ritual for Illumination

Waning Moon: A Ritual for Release

# A Biker Witch's Devotional Practice: Visual Flow

Balanced Engagement: **New Moon Ride** (*see previous*)

**Full Moon Ride**

| Before the Ride |
|:---:|
| ☾ Light a candle to open your ritual. |
| ☾ Call to your ancestors. |
| ☾ Place your offering for them upon your altar. |
| ☾ Tell your ancestors what day and time it is. Share a bit about your day, as if you were speaking with a long-distance friend. |
| ☾ Reflect on the progress you've made toward your intention since the New Moon and on the insights that have come through. |
| ☾ From your heart, ask your ancestors for further clarity and illumination on what nourishes your becoming and what you need to release during the upcoming Waning Moon. Thank your ancestors for their guidance, their love, and their protection. |
| ☾ Leave your offering on the altar for your ancestors to enjoy in your absence, and let them know you will return after your ride. |
| ☾ Gently snuff out your candle, holding the intention of re-lighting it upon your return. |

## During the Ride

C Go for your ride and find a place to sit out.

C Ask the land for permission to be there and feel into whether you're welcome.

C If you are welcome, settle in. If not, keep riding until you find your yes.

C After receiving a yes, let your breath and body become part of the space.

C Call to the spirits of place. Speak or feel your invitation for connection.

C Offer your gratitude in whatever way is asked. You might place a physical offering from your container upon the earth, take a sacred action, or simply be present.

C Introduce yourself. Tell the spirits who you are, why you've come, and how grateful you are to share this time.

C Listen. Witness.

C When you're ready to hit the road again, give thanks.

C Acknowledge the spirits' presence and the time you've shared.

C Close with care. Return your physical offering to the earth, or if your gift is your presence, leave a loving touch on the land as you part.

## The Return

☾ Return to your altar.

☾ Re-light your candle.

☾ Call to your ancestors once more.

☾ Share with your ancestors what you experienced during your ride, offering your reflections as a closing gift.

☾ Thank your ancestors for listening to you and witnessing you today.

☾ Ask them for a dream and tell them when you will return to your altar to connect with them again.

☾ When you're ready, snuff out your candle to close the ritual.

☾ Write in your journal. Record your experiences and any initial impressions or guidance that came through.

☾ Jot down the whole ritual from beginning to end.

☾ Respectfully discard your offerings and take your journal with you to bed.

**Optional:**

Waxing Moon: A Ritual for Deepening

Waning Moon: A Ritual for Release

## Full Flow: Light Engagement

| Moon Phase | Workings |
|---|---|
| New Moon | Devotional Ritual Ride |
| Waxing Moon | A Ritual for Deepening |
| Full Moon | A Ritual for Illumination |
| Waning Moon | A Ritual for Release |

## Full Flow: Balanced Engagement

| Moon Phase | Workings |
|---|---|
| New Moon | Devotional Ritual Ride |
| Waxing Moon | A Ritual for Deepening |
| Full Moon | Devotional Ritual Ride |
| Waning Moon | A Ritual for Release |

# Afterword

Serena had just finished her first read-through of my manuscript when she asked if I planned to include an afterword. In her own wise words, she said that readers should have a moment for an out-breath—a silent, reverent pause after everything they had just experienced.

Admittedly, I knew one was needed, but part of me hoped there was enough said in the body of this book that I wouldn't have to conclude anything. Not because the book doesn't deserve it, or that you, dear reader, shouldn't be held for a moment before dropping your kickstand and turning the key, but because I was so deeply exhausted and unsure of what more I could possibly say.

I also worried that, after two years of grueling devotion to this project, I wouldn't be able to wrap it up and give it the ending it deserves. The thought that my final words might land more like a flatline than a pulsating, reverent moment absolutely terrified me.

I was utterly spent, feeling like I was scraping the bottom of my soul's barrel to find something else to pour into these pages. I decided to turn the moment into an opportunity, not only to try to inspire, but also to be inspired.

I went to my home library, my finger tracing the spines of different books for what felt like hours, until my hand landed on *The Fire Next Time* by James Baldwin. I made a cup of coffee, took a seat on my couch, put my phone on do not disturb, and cracked it open.

I had never read Baldwin's work, though I had watched videos of him. I had seen the sparkle in his eye and heard the ache in his voice. This man was a marvel, and I couldn't believe I had never taken the time to read his words.

It took just the first few sentences for me to become completely captivated. What moved me most was his ability to write every single word with such piercing precision, and yet every syllable was infused with love.

And I mean big love. The kind that leaves you feeling hugged, heartbroken, at peace, and at war all at once.

His words made me think about the importance of art. How it captures history in real time, giving us an archive of the many moments that have shaped where we are today.

I thought about the times I spiraled while writing this book, overwhelmed, thinking, "What's the point? Books are being burned and banned. This world grows more unpredictable every day. What could my words possibly do amid such heaviness?"

Then it hit me. That is the point. There's a reason books are considered a threat. There's a reason art is so heavily policed. I mean, how badass would it be to see piles of *Wheels of Witchcraft* set ablaze? Kinda proving the point of everything this book has been created to combat, right?

Art inspires. It pulls something out of us. It wakes us up in ways we might never have realized we were asleep. That is what James Baldwin did for me in this moment. That is what I hope this book does for you whenever you need it.

Now, I am no James Baldwin. I would never attempt to compare myself to one of the greatest writers of all time. Both writers and riders should always know their limits.

But what I took away was a simple truth: art is a necessary form of playful expression. Not always in the sense of lighthearted fun, but as a tactile way to touch, explore, and move through both our interior and exterior worlds. Even when it confronts serious matters, even when it's heartbreaking, it remains playful, and we simply can't live without it.

Once the word playful entered my mind, I thought about the game of tag I used to play as a kid—the running, the "tag, you're it," and the brief pause at base. Base wasn't a place where we were completely untouched. It was a liminal space in between. A moment to catch our breath, process what was happening, and ready ourselves before stepping back into the unknown.

Art is a lot like that. Someone is "it," sharing their own unique magic from the wellspring of their heart, hoping to touch at least one other soul. Then, once touched, that soul carries that magic forward in their own way, becoming another voice running around the playground.

The chase is the thrill of possibility, the risk of connection, the vulnerability of being seen. Base is the reflective pause between being inspired and inspiring others, the space to process what life has offered, take in what's happening around you, integrate what has been exchanged, and ready yourself for the next run.

The game continues endlessly because the need to connect, to resonate, to be seen, and to see never stops. Even in our most exposed states, in the most tumultuous times, there are safe spaces to return to—books, music, paintings, performances, conversations—places to pause, reflect, and carry that inspiration out into the world again.

Life is an ongoing series of tagging and pausing, chasing and resting, offering and receiving. Like a child laughing as they dart across the playground or gasping as they narrowly make it to base, we are always moving, always feeling, always touching, and always being touched.

In moments like these, when the world feels heavy, when the tide rises and the pendulum swings, when the shadows of fascism and fear creep closer, this movement matters even more.

We ride through the storms together, carrying one another, holding our safe spaces close, and stepping forward when we can.

Maybe that is all this afterword really needs to be: a reminder of the game itself, the playfulness, the love, the exchange, and a whisper that the story doesn't truly end here. It simply passes on to you now.

And perhaps you will be "it" next, running across the open field, calling out to another person who is ready to be touched by what you have to offer.

Biker Witch, thank you for believing in this art, for letting me reach out and share mine, and for daring to make your own magic with it.

May every spell you cast from here forward be infused with a loving, piercing precision.

**Tag, you're it.**

# Acknowledgements

**Caitlin Meyers,** thank you so much for being the best hype woman I could ever ask for. There were moments near the end of this book when I froze up, knowing people would actually be reading it. I knew you were the person to turn to for reassurance, and you delivered. Thank you for being "for the girlies," and for giving this girlie a lifelong friend.

**Krista, Serena, Hex, Raegan, Sabrina, Francesca, Rina, Gabrielle, and Nina,** thank you so much for trusting me to share your stories with the world. Thank you for sharing your heart with the motorcycling community, and for embodying all that makes a Biker Witch so powerful. I feel so lucky to capture your words and usher them into the hearts of so many others. You're all so incredible. Thank you for being a part of this project.

**Chloe Owen,** it has been such an honor to create alongside you, and to see my words adorned and illuminated by your artistry at every step. Thank you for your patience with me through every pivot, change, and revision. I'm so excited for future collaborations with you. Thank you for everything.

**Serena Doyle,** from the moment I decided I was going to self-publish this book, I felt an immediate sense of calmness knowing you would be my editor. I am so grateful you embraced this project and stood beside me as a thought partner and dear friend. Thank you for giving *Wheels of Witchcraft* such a safe first landing, and for shaping it into the book it is today.

**Pixie Lighthorse,** if I could go back and tell my 23-year-old self that one of her favorite writers would one day collaborate with her, she never would have believed it. Having your voice in these pages is a dream come true. Thank you for being in my life, for speaking truth with such clarity, and for adding sparkle and fire to everything you touch. I'm incredibly grateful to call you my friend.

**Tista Wicklow,** thank you for believing in me at every step of this journey. You kept the fire burning when the winds blew, when it rained, and when I felt I had nothing left to say. A conversation with you always reignited the excitement to sit down and keep going. Thank you for being my bestie.

**Maria Patterson,** thank you for showing me what it feels like to have a sister—a woman ready to throw down, show up, laugh, cry, and walk through life with me. I'll never forget the day you looked me in the eyes and said, "You need to stop apologizing so much." That day, you gave me the wake-up I needed to give myself permission to take up space. This book is my own unapologetic way of doing just that. Thank you.

**Haley Daniels,** I honestly, I don't know if I'd still be here on this earth, writing this book, if you hadn't stood so firmly in my corner when I had no one else to turn to. You gave me the tough love I needed and poured love into me when I had none left to give myself. You helped me rebuild my life, and I truly believe you saved it. You are the best friend a woman could ever have. Thank you.

**Sadee Whip,** thank you for *everything.* Your love and guidance have nurtured me into full bloom. Thank you for giving my heart a mirror, my voice a megaphone, and my mind a place to process the past thirty years of my life. Your teachings live within literally every sentence of this book. Thank you for guiding me through the writing process, for hearing my ideas, and for helping me create the outline for this project. This book makes sense because of you—and my life even more so. I love you so much.

**Willow and Anya Redpath-Butler,** thank you for keeping me company on the days I wrote from sunup to sundown. You are the best cat and bird a witch could ever ask for. Thank you for overseeing this entire process and for being the perfect scapegoats if anyone hates this book. If it's too long, too short, too weird, or just plain bad, I will absolutely blame you two for distracting me.

**Marquez Butler,** this book is a testament to the love and unwavering support you've given me over these past two years while writing this book. Thank you for celebrating each milestone, for your patience on the nights I couldn't step away from it, and for making sure I ate and took care of myself along the way. This book exists because of you, because you believed in me even when I didn't, because you carried us financially and emotionally for long stretches so I could write, and because you reminded me again and again that I could keep going. Most of all, thank you for knowing how much this meant to me as a way to share my mother's story. You are the love of my life, and I love you more than words could ever capture.

# Works Consulted

**Quoted Works**

Artisson, Robin. *An Carow Gwyn: Sorcery and the Ancient Fayerie Faith*. Black Malkin Press, 2018.

Artisson, Robin. *The Clovenstone Workings*. Black Malkin Press, 2021.

Frydl, Kathleen. "Readjustment & Postwar Life." *The American Soldier in World War II*, edited by Edward J.K. Gitre, Virginia Tech, 2021, https://americansoldierww2.org/topics/readjustment-and-postwar-life. Accessed 29 Sept. 2024.

Hill, Nancy. "Combat Veterans Tell Us What We Need to Know About War." YES! *Magazine*, 8 Jan. 2020, https://www.yesmagazine.org/social-justice/2020/01/08/war-veterans-military. Accessed 7 Aug. 2024.

Pearce, Lucy H. *Burning Woman*. Womancraft Publishing, 2016.

Whip, Sadee. *Savage Awakening: Initiatory Paths of the Dragon Mother*. Dragon Mother Media, 2023.

Wolynn, Mark. *It Didn't Start With You: How Inherited Family Trauma Shapes Who We Are and How to End the Cycle*. Penguin Books, 2017.

Women's Refugee Commission. *Women on the Run: First-Hand Accounts of Refugees Fleeing El Salvador, Guatemala, Honduras, and Mexico.* Women's Refugee Commission, 2015. Web. https://www.womensrefugeecommission.org/reports/women-on-the-run/.

## Other Consulted Works

Amnesty International. *Why is the Democratic Republic of Congo Wracked by Conflict?* Amnesty International, 2024. Web. www.amnesty.org/en/latest/campaigns/why-is-the-democratic-republic-of-congo-wracked-by-conflict/

Angus, Ian. *The War Against the Commons.* NYU Press, 2023.

Bloch, Marc. *Feudal Society.* Routledge & Kegan Paul, 1961.

Braudel, Fernand. *Civilization and Capitalism, 15th–18th Century.* Vol. I, Harper & Row, 1982.

Center for Economic and Social Rights (CEOBS). *The Environmental Costs of the War in Sudan.* CEOBS, 2023. Web. https://ceobs.org/the-environmental-costs-of-the-war-in-sudan/.

Crawley, Ashon T., and Roberto Sirvent, editors. *Spirituality and Abolition.* Common Notions, 2023.

DePastino, Todd. "Why Veterans Love Motorcycles." *Veterans Breakfast Club,* 8 Jan. 2020, https://www.veteransbreakfastclub.org/why-veterans-love-motorcycles. Accessed 7 Aug. 2024.

Desai, Chandni. "Disrupting Settler-Colonial Capitalism: Indigenous Intifadas and Resurgent Solidarity from Turtle Island to Palestine." *Journal of Palestine Studies,* 2022. Web. https://www.palestine-studies.org/en/node/1651274.

Estés, Clarissa Pinkola. *Women Who Run with the Wolves: Myths and Stories of the Wild Woman Archetype.* Ballantine Books, 1992.

Federici, Silvia. *Caliban and the Witch: Women, the Body and Primitive Accumulation.* Autonomedia, 2004.

Indigenous Climate Action. "Indigenous Women Stand in Solidarity with Palestine." Indigenous Climate Action, 2023. Web. https://www.indigenousclimateaction.com/entries/solidarity-humanitarian-flotilla.

Inikori, Joseph E. *The Atlantic Slave Trade: Effects on Economies, Societies, and Peoples in Africa, the Americas, and Europe.* Duke University Press, 2010.

Knight, Alex. "Who Were the Witches? Patriarchal Terror and the Creation of Capitalism." *The End of Capitalism*, 5 Nov. 2009, https://endofcapitalism.com/2009/11/05/who-were-the-witches-patriarchal-terror-and-the-creation-of-capitalism/. Accessed 30 Sept. 2024.

Mongabay. "Cobalt Mining for Green Energy Risks Women's Reproductive Health in DRC." Mongabay, 2024. Web. https://news.mongabay.com/2024/11/cobalt-mining-for-green-energy-risks-womens-reproductive-health-in-drc/

National WWII Museum. "Great Responsibilities and New Global Power: The National WWII Museum: New Orleans." *The National WWII Museum | New Orleans*, 23 Oct. 2020, https://www.nationalww2museum.org/war/articles/new-global-power-after-world-war-ii-1945. Accessed 7 Aug. 2024.

Stoler, Ann Laura. *Carnal Knowledge and Imperial Power: Race and the Intimate in Colonial Rule.* University of California Press, 2002.

Vesta, Lara Veleda. *Wild Soul Runes: Reawakening the Ancestral Feminine.* Red Wheel/Weiser, 2021.

Zinn, Howard, and Anthony Arnove. *A People's History of the United States.* 35th anniversary ed., HarperPerennial, 2015.

# About Rhiannon

Rhiannon Redpath is a writer, chopper-builder, and witch who moves with the seasons between the Pacific Northwest and New Orleans, Louisiana.

Writing, whether as a skill, a passion, or a profession, wasn't on her radar until a college creative writing class, when a professor elevated one of her poems to the class, giving her the confidence and encouragement to find her voice.

Carrying significant personal trauma, it was only in recent years that she has found the language to fully express what lives in her heart, and now she simply can't shut up about it.

With a Bachelor of Science in Human Development from Virginia Tech, Rhiannon gained a deep understanding of how our traumas and personal stories shape the way we think, move through community, and connect with others.

This knowledge informed her work as a full-spectrum doula, where she learned to hold space for life's most pivotal moments while navigating the intersection of systemic structures and individual experience.

She became adept at protecting each person's unique journey from unnecessary systemic disruptions, creating safe and supportive spaces for transformation. Today, this ability to bridge the structural and the personal informs every aspect of her work.

After building her chopper and running her doula practice full time, Rhiannon discovered surprising commonalities between the garage and the birthing space. The creativity, adrenaline, and other fateful forces that flow through both inspired her to merge these paths into a single offering for her community.

Guided by her mother's legacy, she found a way to bridge the worlds of motorcycling and witchcraft. This became the heart of her witchcraft practice and the foundation of the Motherline Magic Moto Coven—a space where individual magic is honored, stories are held sacred, and collective power thrives.

**Instagram:** thechopperwitch & motherlinemagic
**Website:** www.motherlinemagic.com

# ABOUT SERENA

Serena Doyle lives in beautiful Herefordshire, where she has spent the last 25 years raising her family.

Serena has always adored words. Growing up, she would often read a novel in a day, and would write pages and pages in letters to her friends, proofreading and editing their replies (much to her current dismay!).

She studied English and English literature at school with great enthusiasm, and then carried this on in college. But it wasn't until later, after her years as a full-time homemaker, and then Early Years teacher, that she revisited writing and editing, earning her Diploma with the College of Media and Publishing.

Since then, she has volunteered her time and skills to help women-led businesses gain traction, through writing and optimizing articles and blog posts, rewriting websites, and developing email marketing strategies. Serena has a real passion for collaboration, and for supporting spaces where women feel safe to shine.

Her work with Rhiannon on *Wheels of Witchcraft* has been just that—a collaborative process as an editor, a thought partner, and a copywriter. The way in which she works highlights the deep awe and respect she has for her fellow creatives, writers, and thinkers.

**Instagram:** s.rena_d
**Website:** https://serenadoyle.co.uk

# ABOUT CHLOE

Chloe Owen is a graphic designer and illustrator located in Southern California. She is a former BFA student of Chapman University, where she studied Graphic Design and Environmental Sciences.

Not only has Chloe had a deep connection to art from a young age, but she has also always felt a calling to nature. She strives to incorporate both of these passions in her work, whether that be in subject matter, sourcing inspiration, or choosing to work with like-minded small businesses and creators.

Chloe rejoices in working off-screen as well, whether that be painting on motorcycle tanks, helmets, cowboy hats, mirrors, bandanas, and more. In all of her creative outlets, she pulls most of her inspiration from vintage designs dating back to Victorian Era prints, Western and Americana culture, 70s motorcycle lifestyle, as well as traditional tattoo art.

When she's not working, you can find her riding her 1974 Ironhead Sportster, seeing live music, spending time outdoors, hanging with her two cats, or spending quality time with family and loved ones.

**Instagram:** chlointhedarkdesigns

# About Pixie

Cherie Dawn Carr is a tribal member of the Choctaw Nation of Oklahoma. She writes as Lighthorse to honor the unheard voices of her ancestors, has published seven books of healing and prayers, works daily in land and food justice, and is mother of two.

Her paternal grandparents were Choctaw, and her great-grandmother was enrolled Cherokee. Due to the Dawes Act of 1887, which aimed to dissolve and redistribute her ancestors' tribal lands, individuals could only be claimed by one Nation for a brief but strategic period in colonial time.

Her heavy Irish descendancy means that in one body lives the memories of the first peoples England colonized in the 12th century combined with the most recently colonized peoples on Turtle Island. The Choctaw and the other southeastern "civilized tribes" were the first Natives officially removed from their home places and into Indian Territory now known as Oklahoma.

Lighthorse believes that knowing when our ancestors' bodies were colonized by Rome or England is very important for medicine makers and healers of all walks in order to undo the damage perpetrated on all Indigenous peoples.

She maintains that magic is the act of transforming one reality into another and that motorcycles were born of rebellious spiritedness, a willingness to take risks and make loud statements about how we get from here to there. She teaches that when we combine strong ancestral knowledge with strong medicines, magic helps us get to where we're going: prayers up, wheels down.

**Website:** www.pixielighthorse.com

# Join Our Coven

The Motherline Magic Moto Coven is a global sisterhood of Biker Witches. Rooted in New Orleans, our magic flows outward, crossing oceans and reaching women in every corner of the world. Our sisters come from all walks of life, each bringing their own unique culture, traditions, and stories  into this revolutionary web we're weaving.

The coven grows every day, bound by a love for the ride and this journey of self-discovery that connects us. You're welcome to join us in gathering around the experiences sparked by this book and sharing how you carry them back into your life. We meet in person, online, and in all the mysterious places where magic and motorcycles merge.

**Instagram:** motherlinemagic
**Website:** www.motherlinemagic.com